6.38

Foreword by
PHEME PERKINS

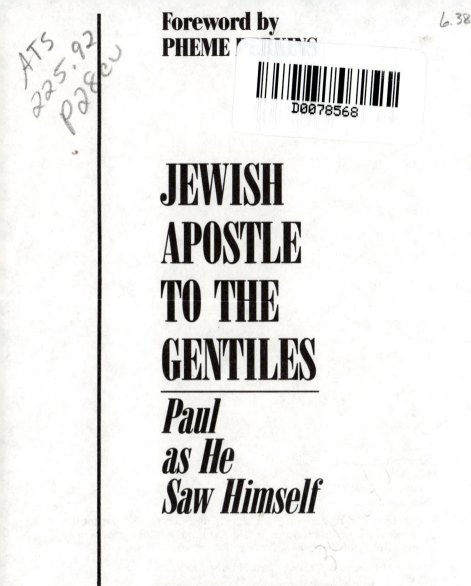

JEWISH APOSTLE TO THE GENTILES

Paul as He Saw Himself

PHILIP A. CUNNINGHAM

TWENTY-THIRD PUBLICATIONS
Mystic, Connecticut

16225

Twenty-Third Publications
P.O. Box 180
Mystic, CT 06355
(203) 536-2611

Library of Congress Catalog Card Number 86-50236
ISBN 0-89622-302-7

Edited and designed by Helen Coleman
Cover design by Kathy Michalove
Cover Art: The St. Paul figure on the cover resides in the narthex of St. Patrick's Cathedral in New York City. The photograph is used with the kind permission of Msgr. James F. Rigney, rector of St. Patrick's Cathedral. The sculptor of this figure and of a companion figure of St. Peter, also at St. Patrick's, is Adlai S. Hardin. The cover photo is by George W. Potts.

JEWISH APOSTLE TO THE GENTILES
Paul as He Saw Himself

"At long last the truth about Paul begins to prevail, that he never became a Christian, but remained a devout Jew all his life; that he never converted, but obeyed a call; that his undivided love went out both to his fellow Jews and his Gentile converts; that most of his theology is based upon rabbinic trains of thought and, last but not least, that his only Holy Writ was the Jewish Bible, upon which he built his hope for redemption and his undying message of ecumenical love.

Judaism and Christianity are certainly different ways to the One God, but need they be contrastive, antagonistic, or antithetical? Should we Jews not have a closer look at this admittedly controversial zealot, who had his own ideas about salvation, exegesis, and missionary work?

What ultimately counts is his message to the Romans: 'For as many as are led by the Spirit of God, these are children of God' (Romans 8:14). I do hope Cunningham's book will help stimulate the Christian-Jewish dialogue."

Pinchas Lapide
co-author of *Paul, Rabbi and Apostle*

Lovingly dedicated to My Father,
Hugh A. Cunningham,
whose love for learning was contagious

Acknowledgments

Like most of the activities of the Salem Christian Life Center, this book is in some ways the result of a team effort. The following people deserve much thanks for all their work in proof-reading the manuscript through its various incarnations, in making extremely helpful suggestions, and in aiding in the development of the Questions for Reflection and Discussion:

> Mrs. Teresa V. Baker
> Mr. Hugh J. Cunningham
> Mr. Joseph Goergen
> Mrs. Michelle Labonte
> Mrs. Donna Mannarini
> Mrs. Joyce Rollins

There are also other special people who have provided invaluable aid. I express my deepest gratitude to:

Mr. Leon E. Abbott, Jr. for his aid in preparing the scriptural index, and especially for his keen insights in our long conversations together which clarified many of the theological points presented in this book.

Msgr. John F. Barry for examining the completed manuscript and for enthusiastically encouraging its publication.

Very Rev. Karl F. Dowd, V.F., dean of the Salem Deanery, for generously providing virtually unlimited access to Word Processing equipment, thereby reducing the work of years down to months.

Prof. David P. Efroymson, of LaSalle University in Philadelphia, for his assistance in reviewing the final manuscript.

Ms. Julia Anne Walsh, my wife, who was the prime mover behind this book's development, and who constantly supported and affirmed its composition with steadfast love.

Foreword

This book insists upon the need for average Christians to understand the results of modern biblical research. The author rightly points out that study of the Bible today is aided by advances in sciences like archaeology and linguistics and in a knowledge of ancient history that was not available even half a century ago. Christians who neglect to make such results part of their faith are as foolish as persons who would refuse to drive an automobile, use modern medicines, or in other ways reject the world of the twentieth century. We are all capable of understanding about new developments in fields like medicine, economics, and even engineering without being masters of any of those fields. Our knowledge of the Bible should be no different.

This book has been tested in work with adult groups. The author has also digested the best in modern scholarship through his own reading and study. The book's opening chapter gives the reader a quick tour through the emergence of the early Christian movement from Jesus' mission in Galilee through the churches outside Palestine which Paul had first persecuted and then joined as their best known apostle.

The central theme of the book is to recapture the "Jewishness" of Christianity. His Holiness, Pope Paul II, has reaffirmed the importance of that theme for Catholics in his historic visit to a synagogue in Rome. There the Pontiff greeted members of the Jewish community as our "elder brothers." This study of Paul's letters shows how deep those roots are. Paul's calling to preach Christ among the Gentiles did not cut him off from the faith of his fathers. But Paul saw that God had done a "gracious" deed, which actually brought all the promises of the Covenant with Israel to perfection. Through faith in Christ, God has summoned the non-Jews into fellowship. They need no longer be enemies, cut off from God, but can be beloved children of God.

Cunningham rightly insists that first century Jews experienced the Law (Torah) as a gracious gift, not an enslaving power. He shows that when Paul argues against the enslavement of persons to the Law, he is referring to Christians (some of them converted Gentiles) who thought that the Jewish way of life would have to be imposed upon the Gentiles if they were to receive salvation in Christ. Paul is not telling Christians of Jewish heritage that they have to give up their traditional way of life in order to believe in Jesus as Messiah. However, Paul appears to have foreseen the danger that an all Gentile church might forget and turn against its Jewish heritage (Romans 9-11). We are in the process of trying to heed Paul's warnings!

One of the most important elements in the Jewish faith is the requirement that persons live a life of holiness and faithfulness to God. The chapter on living "in Christ" shows how Paul has used this insight to instruct his non-Jewish converts that they must live according to the "Law of Christ." Following Jewish patterns sexual misconduct is associated with idolatry, turning away from God. Another major category of moral teaching concerns the virtues that are necessary for persons to live together in harmonious community. The Christian community must always seek to shape its relationships in terms of the love and sacrifice which it sees embodied in Christ. These same principles are also demonstrated by the life of the apostle. Christ, for Paul, is the "new Adam," the example of the way in which God intended human beings to live. Thus, Christian morality does not look to a legal code or even to the Law from which it draws many of its ethical insights. Christian morality always looks directly to the example that has been given in Christ.

This book is a thoughtful and able presentation of Paul, the Jewish apostle. It has drawn upon the best in modern scholarship and grapples with an issue that remains an important one for Christians today. Though aimed at Roman Catholics, this book might also serve as the basis for ecumenical study groups of different Christian denominations or of Christians and Jews.

PHEME PERKINS
BOSTON COLLEGE

Contents

JEWISH APOSTLE TO THE GENTILES
Paul as He Saw Himself

Introduction

It has become common knowledge that a virtual revolution in Bible scholarship has been underway for several decades. There is also a widespread public interest in the Scriptures, and various types of Bible study programs are flourishing. Despite these facts, it appears that as yet relatively few people have benefited from the tremendous insights garnered by modern scriptural research. Paradoxically, at a time when there is a heightened curiosity about the Bible, there seems to be an equally widespread lack of awareness of the profound fruits of recent critical investigations into the Scriptures.

In particular, there have recently been enormous developments in scholarly understanding of the letters of the apostle Paul. For centuries, Paul has been understood as someone who had renounced his Jewish heritage, who had become a zealous Christian missionary, who had attacked the supposed Jewish belief that one earned salvation through works of the Law, and who insisted instead on justification by faith. Current Bible research, however, is revealing that such a view may be largely based on erroneous assumptions about Paul and about his Jewish heritage. It is beginning to become apparent that far from being an opponent of Judaism, Paul was a faithful Jew throughout his life and defined his mission in Christ exclusively in terms of his gospel to the Gentiles. But these new perspectives, like the modern biblical movement itself, have yet to be widely appreciated by the general public.

This book has been written for the general reader who

is somewhat acquainted with Paul's letters. It aims to present the new and thought-provoking insights into Paul which some contemporary research has produced. Furthermore, it will seek to offer suggestions about a few currently unresolved issues in Pauline scholarship. On the interpretation of certain disputed passages there is still a lack of scholarly consensus. Nonetheless, although on certain details there is room for debate, this book will attempt to show that an overall approach to Paul which respects his Jewish traditions is not only possible, but is required by the biblical texts. Hopefully, this presentation of recent work on Paul's Jewishness will be made in a clear, untechnical manner in good old everyday English.

The format to be followed herein roughly corresponds to a six-week introduction to Paul program offered by the Salem Deanery Christian Life Center in southern New Hampshire. The approximately three hundred participants in this program have not only served to "field-test" the materials used in this book, but several of them have assisted the author in being sensitive to the use of excessive technical jargon and in developing the discussion and reflection questions at the end of each chapter.

It is hoped that readers of this book might be encouraged to consult some of the references which will be given as a means of deepening their appreciation of the Bible. To avoid cluttering pages with the footnotes for such references, all citations will be in the form of endnotes at the conclusion of the book. Some of these endnotes will recommend books for further reading, while others will be citations of current scholarly works. Any comments at the bottom of a page (which will be indicated by asterisks [*]) will be for explanatory remarks only.

Each chapter is followed by the previously mentioned discussion and reflection questions which are meant to relate the chapter to the current twentieth-century situation, and which can be used either by individuals or by discussion groups. Also, at the end of the book will be found an Index of Scriptural Passages. While every single word of Paul's letters will not be addressed, this index may be helpful as one reads an individual Pauline letter. By locating in the index the particular chapter and verse being explored, the reader will be referred to the page where that passage is discussed.

As this encounter with Paul begins, it might be well to note that Paul's letters were not addressed to modern-day Christians. They were all written by a first-century man to a first-century audience. This fact will be the guiding principle behind this undertaking. To really hear Paul's message, we must try to read his words from the perspective of first-century Jewish or Gentile followers of Jesus. By hearing Paul's words according to *his* first-century concepts and frames of reference, and by discarding subsequent Christian stereotypes of Judaism, his message becomes not only clear, but also uncomfortably challenging and surprisingly significant for today's world and church.

CHAPTER ONE

Paul and His Era

THE MODERN BIBLICAL MOVEMENT

Although many people are aware that Bible scholars are arriving at dramatic new insights into the scriptures, it may not be so widely understood why such changes are happening now (or even why there are any changes at all!). Haven't we had the word of God in the scriptures for hundreds of years? Why should twentieth-century Bible readers understand the sacred writings in any different ways than previous generations? To refer to the subject of this book, why should scholars be coming to different conclusions about the apostle Paul?

An initial response to these kinds of questions can be seen in the numerous archaeological discoveries of the past century. Important finds like those in Nag Hammadi, Egypt (1945) or in the caves along the Dead Sea (1947) have provided us with literature written around the same time as the New Testa-

ment scriptures. In addition, the unearthing of documents written in the same dialect as New Testament Greek—called *koine*
(koy-nay) or "common" Greek—has enabled translators to
render early Christian writings with greater accuracy.[1] Similar
increased access to Jewish writings of the first and second centuries is also having a tremendous impact on our understanding
of the origins of the Christian gospel. For example, the parables
of Jesus can be seen to have even more profound meanings
than previously realized when they are set in the context of
Jesus' Jewish heritage.[2] Or as another example, it is becoming
increasingly clear that Paul can only be properly understood
when his Pharisaic heritage is appreciated.

This leads to the other major spark of the modern
biblical movement. At the same time as major archaeological
and language treasures were being unearthed, there was also
a growing awareness that to understand the Bible correctly one
had to try to determine why a particular sacred author was
writing and what that writer was trying to say. Using Paul
as an illustration, why did he write letters to Corinth? What
was going on there that caused him to react? What training
or experiences in Paul's life might have caused him to think
or conceive of his faith in certain ways? How did people write
and express themselves in the first century? How did Paul?
What was happening historically when Paul wrote and how
did those events influence him?

All of these questions aim at putting the sacred writers
in the *context* of their time, culture, and experience in order
to perceive their inspired message clearly. Most Christian
denominations now agree that the Bible's meaning can only
be arrived at after one has *first* discerned what the biblical
authors were trying to tell *their own contemporaries*. The
Roman Catholic tradition expresses the thought in this way:

> However, since God speaks in sacred Scriptures
> through men in human fashion, the interpreter of
> sacred Scripture, in order to see clearly what God
> wanted to communicate to us, should carefully in-
> vestigate what meaning the sacred writers really in-
> tended, and what God wanted to manifest by means
> of their words....The interpreter must investigate

what meaning the sacred writer intended to express...as he used contemporary literary forms in accordance with the situation of his own time and culture. For the correct understanding of what the sacred author wanted to assert, due attention must be paid to the customary and characteristic styles of perceiving, speaking, and narrating which prevailed at the time of the sacred writer, and to the customs men normally followed at that period in their everyday dealings with one another.[3]

This statement captures the essence of the modern biblical approach—an approach that can be called the historical-critical method. It is historical because it seeks to understand a sacred writer, such as Paul, as a person situated in and affected by history. It is critical because it seeks to distinguish between various cultural influences and divine revelation.[4]

Modern scriptural awareness holds that the Bible is the word of God but is written by human beings in human languages, and that these human writers need to be appreciated as conditioned by their heritages, cultures, and eras.[5]

To summarize, the current advances in Bible scholarship could only have happened in our time because of the exciting archaeological discoveries of recent decades, and because of the critical tools that can reveal the various forces and processes which influenced the sacred writers. More profoundly, the changes in our appreciation of the scriptures demonstrate that the body of Christ is a living organism which is continuously growing in its understanding of the word of God.

Before applying these methods and discoveries to Paul, a brief outline of the events which occurred before he became a follower of Jesus might be helpful.

THE MOVEMENT PAUL JOINED

Paul eventually became a participant in what had originally been a renewal movement within Judaism begun around the year 30. It had been inspired by a Jew named Jesus who came from the town of Nazareth in the region called Galilee, about seventy-five miles north of Jerusalem.

Both northern Galilee and the southern province of Judea (whose capital was Jerusalem) had been under the domination of the Roman Empire for about three-quarters of a century. Although the Temple leaders in Jerusalem collaborated with Rome in order to keep the peace, Galilee was a virtual hotbed of revolution against the Roman occupation. By the time of Jesus there had been decades of violence against the Romans perpetrated by Galilean rebels.[6] These Galilean "resistance fighters" had little love for the Temple collaborationists whom they considered traitors to Israel.[7]

The movement Jesus started appears to have initially been a purely rural phenomenon. The gospels, for instance, make frequent mention of farmers, fishermen, shepherds, and vine-growers, but few words appear about urban craftsmen or merchants.[8] References in the gospels to the accents characteristic of Jesus' followers (Mt. 26:73) and remarks such as "can anything good come out of Nazareth?" (Jn. 1:46) demonstrate not only the essentially Galilean nature of the Jesus movement, but also the low regard in which the inhabitants of Jerusalem held their northern kinsfolk.

Obviously it is beyond the scope of this book to detail current scholarly reconstructions of the historical ministry of Jesus, but perhaps the following will be sufficient:*

It is clear from the Gospels of Mark, Matthew, and Luke that Jesus acted with the utmost conviction that the Reign of God—that ultimate ordering of all creation to God's will— was about to break into human history. He seems to have deliberately sought to build a reinvigorated People of Israel united in loving forgiveness and healed of all their divisions.[9] He taught a radically intensified Torah** which promised recon-

---

* Readers may notice in the following paragraphs an absence of divine titles applied to Jesus. Modern scriptural research is indicating that such elevated views about Jesus did not arise until after his death and resurrection. Post-resurrectional insights into the presence of God in Jesus did not occur during his ministry and, consequently, cannot be included in a historical reconstruction of that ministry. For more information on this point see the statement issued in 1964 by the Roman Catholic Pontifical Biblical Commission entitled *The Historical Truth of the Gospels*. This document details the three time periods which can be detected in the gospels: the ministry of Jesus; the post-resurrection years; and the time of the evangelist.

** The "Torah" was and is the Law of the Jewish people, sometimes called the Law

ciliation not only among all Jews, but eventually even with the Gentiles (including the Romans!).[10] By means of heart-touching parables, by signs demonstrating the power of God at work correcting evils and injustices, and by table-fellowship with outcasts, Jesus sought to assemble this renewed Israel—an Israel fully prepared and eagerly participating in the inbreaking of God's universal Reign.[11]

Jesus eventually brought this renewal movement to the Jewish capital itself. There his enemies among the Romans and the Temple leadership succeeded in publicly executing him by the Roman torture of crucifixion as an insurrectionist "King of the Jews." Jesus' agonizing death in public disgrace may have occurred in April of the year 33.[12]

Shortly thereafter Jesus' followers, who had abandoned their leader and possibly had returned home to Galilee,[13] reappeared in Jerusalem claiming that God had raised Jesus from death and had thereby divinely vindicated Jesus' policies and activities. A community of Jews who now claimed Jesus as their "Lord" assembled, and began to spread their "Good News" throughout the city and even in the Temple.

In this community were both native Hebrew-speaking Palestinian Jews and also Jews from elsewhere in the Roman Empire whose native language was Greek. It appears that before long these Hellenistic* followers of Jesus became embroiled in a violent conflict with the Temple authorities, and one of them named Stephen was stoned to death. The Palestinian (Hebrew-speaking) Jesus followers do not seem to have been directly affected by these hostilities and they continued to pray in the Temple and to celebrate their worship of the Raised Lord's supper unmolested.[15] However, the Hellenistic Jesus followers fled Jerusalem. They and Jesus followers from Galilee began preaching about the raising of Jesus in Samaria,[16]

---

of Moses. In a specific sense it is the first five books of the Bible, although it can be understood more broadly as the entire body of Jewish sacred writings. The Torah defines the lifestyle by which Jews respond to God's gracious gift of Covenant with them. As will be seen, the English term "law" does not fully express all the meanings connoted by Torah. The word "way" might be better.[14]

---

* "Hellenistic" Jews are simply Jews from outside Palestine whose native tongue was Greek. They may or may not have spoken Hebrew also.

in Antioch, and perhaps by the mid-40s in Rome itself.[17]

It was this initial preaching of the Gospel to Jews who lived outside of Palestine that brought the name of Jesus the Christ* to the ears of large numbers of Gentiles. To fully appreciate how such Gentiles would perceive the Jewish Jesus movement, it is necessary to understand what Gentiles thought of the Jews who lived in their midst.

Over the course of time large numbers of Jews had established their residency in widely scattered areas of the Empire.[18] Living far away from Jerusalem they naturally did not see the Temple as the most important feature in their religious lives. Instead their spirituality revolved around the local synagogue and the Torah.[19] There were large Jewish populations in Babylon, Alexandria, Corinth, Rome, and in all the major cities. One population estimate indicates that in the first half of the first century there were about 2.5 million (and possibly as few as 800,000) Jews living in Palestine, while about 4.5 million Jews lived elsewhere in the Empire.[20] In other words, there were almost twice as many Jews living outside Palestine as there were living inside.

Such "scattered" or "Diaspora" Jews became familiar with the customs of the Gentiles among whom they lived. Some adopted Greco-Roman hairstyles, dress, names, languages, and citizenship. Yet there still was a basic Jewish rejection of the blatant sexuality in Greek society generally, and in Greek religious practices in particular.[21]

Gentiles had both positive and negative opinions of their Jewish neighbors. From the Gentile viewpoint, Jews were to be criticized for their "strangeness." At a time when the so-called "Roman peace" offered the possibility of a unified culture for most the known world, Jews obstinately refused to surrender their self-identity as a special people.[22] They stubbornly clung to their "odd" ethnic and dietary customs, they refused to acknowledge the legitimacy of Greek deities, they tended toward clannishness and generally married only within their own people. Furthermore, even though their homeland in

---

* "Christ" is Greek for "anointed one" and is roughly equivalent to the Hebrew "Messiah," God's "Chosen One" or agent who would be instrumental in ushering in the Reign of God.

Palestine was a rebellious and troublesome region, the Jews still managed to obtain from Julius Caesar a dispensation from having to worship Roman gods. [23]

On the other hand, Judaism was found to be quite appealing by some Gentiles. Its strong moral code, the loyalty and faithfulness of Jews toward one another, and the covenanted worship of one supreme God may all have been considered attractive features of Judaism. [24] One first-century writer noted that in Antioch Jews "were constantly attracting to their religious ceremonies multitudes of Greeks, and these they had in some measure incorporated with themselves." [25]

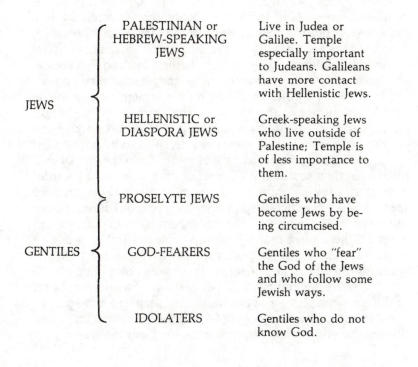

JEWS	PALESTINIAN or HEBREW-SPEAKING JEWS	Live in Judea or Galilee. Temple especially important to Judeans. Galileans have more contact with Hellenistic Jews.
	HELLENISTIC or DIASPORA JEWS	Greek-speaking Jews who live outside of Palestine; Temple is of less importance to them.
GENTILES	PROSELYTE JEWS	Gentiles who have become Jews by being circumcised.
	GOD-FEARERS	Gentiles who "fear" the God of the Jews and who follow some Jewish ways.
	IDOLATERS	Gentiles who do not know God.

This "incorporation" refers to Gentiles who did not become Jews by being circumcised, but who nevertheless became sort of semi-Jewish by observing Jewish Sabbath and holyday rituals, by participating in synagogue services, and possibly by following some dietary customs. These semi-Jewish Gentiles are frequently called the "God-fearers"; people who knew the God of Abraham, Isaac, and Jacob, and who minimally observed the Jewish Torah. [26] There is also evidence that Judaism was so attractive to certain Gentiles that they actually "converted" to Judaism by being circumcised. There were evidently enough of these converts or "proselytes" to provoke Roman imperial decrees to discourage such conversions. [27]

With this background it now becomes possible to reconstruct the probable course of events as the first followers of Jesus began arriving in the various Gentile cities. These Jews who believed in Jesus as Lord would begin preaching to their fellow Jews in the local synagogue. Their words would also be heard by the God-fearing Gentiles of the community. It appears that these God-fearers were greatly attracted by this preaching, probably because some of the early Christ-preachers permitted the Gentiles to join the movement without being circumcised as a Jew but by merely being baptized. [28] There is also growing evidence that the early gospel was very appealing to women. Rather than having their membership in the saved community contingent upon their father's or husband's circumcision as in Judaism, now they could be part of the church of Jesus based on their own decision to be baptized. [29]

At any rate, it is clear that by the 40s in the city of Antioch in Syria a significant number of un-circumcised Gentiles were permitted to enter the Jesus-movement. This practice seems to have occurred spontaneously without having been discussed by the leaders of the movement beforehand, and apparently there were many believers who did not approve of what was starting to happen. Especially among the Hebrew-speaking members in Jerusalem there was complaint. [30]

Sometime in the late 30s or early 40s Paul became part of this growing Jesus-movement, and he seems to have played a major role in the debates over Gentile membership. This question of the admissions requirements for Gentiles was a very divisive one. Eventually, a gathering of leaders of the Jesus movement was held in Jerusalem to settle the matter. This meeting has been called either the Apostolic Council or the Council of Jerusalem, and probably occurred around the year 50.[31]

Among those participating in this Council were Peter, Paul, and James. It seems that the meeting decided that Gentiles could become members of the church (or assembly) of Jesus without becoming Jews by circumcision first. This decision was to have far-reaching consequences.

By the time of Paul's death in the 60s, the Jesus-movement was becoming predominantly Gentile in its membership. This trend was given added impetus by the Jewish-Roman War which lasted between the years 66 and 70. When the Romans destroyed Jerusalem and leveled the Temple in the year 70 the Jerusalem church was also ended, leaving the Jesus-movement even more of a Gentile phenomenon.[32]

It may have been noticed that in this discussion the use of the word "Christian" has been avoided. This is because the term did not arise until the 80s, by which time the church was not only mostly Gentile, but was also becoming more and more distant from Judaism. That was not the situation during the years of Paul's activities (40s - 60s). In Paul's time the majority of believers in Jesus as Lord were Jews, and the term "Jesus-movement" will be used to reflect this fact. The initial Jesus-movement was predominantly Jewish, later "Christianity" was mostly Gentile.[33]

An overall picture of the events described above might be seen more clearly by listing them in a chronological table:[34]

A CHRONOLOGY OF THE FIRST CENTURY

31(?)-33   Ministry of Jesus.

33   The crucifixion and death of Jesus and the resurrection. Beginning of Jerusalem church and the death of Stephen. Spreading of Jesus-movement by Hellenistic and Galilean Jews.

34-35	The calling of Paul as apostle to the Gentiles. He begins preaching in Syria and Cilicia.
early 40s	Gentiles are baptized into the church at Antioch without being circumcised first.
early-mid 40s	Founding of a church at Rome?
early 40s	Barnabas makes Paul's acquaintance and introduces him to the thriving church at Antioch. For the next several years they journey together in Asia Minor founding many churches which apparently admit uncircumcised Gentiles.
50	Council of Jerusalem meets. Church leaders formally ratify policy regarding the admission of Gentiles without circumcision.
50	In Antioch, Paul accuses Peter of hypocrisy in a dispute over dietary practices. Paul departs and begins a great missionary journey throughout Greece. The procedure for Jewish and Gentile table-fellowship is eventually worked out by having Gentiles observe certain minimal standards.
51-58	The writing of Paul's letters to the various churches, probably in this order: 1 Thessalonians, Galatians, Philippians, the letters to Corinth, Philemon, and Romans.*
58	Paul journeys to Jerusalem with the collection from the Gentile churches. He is arrested by the Romans and eventually taken to Rome for a legal decision.

---

* Note that Paul's letters pre-date the writing of the gospels by decades. They are the oldest parts of the New Testament. For this reason they are a source of very early Christian thought and do not contain certain of the theological reflections which occurred in later years.

62-64	Executions of both Paul and Peter in Rome.
66	Outbreak of the Jewish-Roman War.
70	Destruction of Jerusalem and the Temple. End of the Jerusalem church.
70	Writing of the Gospel of Mark.
80s	Gradual separation between the increasingly Gentile church and Judaism; use of the term "Christian" becomes popular.
85	The Gospels of Luke and Matthew are written, independently of each other.
80s	Writing of Ephesians and Colossians?
90	Meeting of the Council of Javneh at which the surviving Jewish leadership defines post-Temple Judaism along Rabbinic lines.
95	Writing of Gospel of John.
100	Writing of 1 and 2 Timothy, and Titus.

And so we have seen that a Jewish renewal movement begun by a Jew from Galilee met with apparent disaster in the Judean capital of Jerusalem. However, with its founder later proclaimed as the Raised Lord it was spread by Hellenistic Jews to their fellow-Jews elsewhere in the Roman Empire, and at the same time to Gentile God-fearers. Such Gentiles came to dominate the movement, eventually called Christianity. Paul apparently contributed much to this gradual "Gentilization" of the Jesus-movement, and, with this background, we shall now turn to the available sources of information about him.

GETTING TO KNOW PAUL

Following the principles outlined so far, it is clear that an encounter with Paul must begin by asking questions about his "life and times." What sources of information about Paul are available? What kind of person was he? What happened to him during his lifetime?

The primary sources of information about Paul are obviously the letters which he wrote to various church communities, roughly between the years 50 and 60. There is wide scholarly agreement that Paul himself composed the letters we have come to know as 1 Thessalonians, Galatians, Philippians, 2 Corinthians, Philemon, and Romans. These seven "authentic letters" of Paul will be the principal means of getting to know Paul.[35]

A major secondary source of information is the New Testament book called Acts of Apostles. Written around the year 85 by an admirer of Paul, it corroborates some of the information gleaned from the letters. In some passages, though, Acts seems more reflective of its author's opinions *about* Paul rather than being accurate remembrances of opinions *of* Paul. At such places where Acts and the letters disagree (such as the respective accounts of the "Council of Jerusalem"), the letters must be considered more reliable sources of information about Paul.

Finally, some indirect access to Paul can be obtained from letters written in Paul's name by his disciples after his death. Although apparently attributed to Paul, there is widespread scholarly agreement that Ephesians, Colossians, and most definitely 1 Timothy, 2 Timothy, and Titus were written later on in the first century. (The debate over 2 Thessalonians is less resolved, but for our purposes it will be included with these other "deutero-Pauline"* writings.)[36] That disciples would write in their master's name after his death should not be shocking or thought of as some kind of forgery (a twentieth century notion). Such "pseudonymous" writing was quite commonplace, and was considered a way of honoring and preserving the master's legacy. Furthermore, the belief that 1 Timothy, for example, was not written by Paul in no way compromises its spiritual value. It is the author's message, not his identity, that is important. In fact, we are ignorant of the identities of most of the sacred writers, Paul's authentic letters being something of an exception.

At any rate, it is the authentically Pauline letters that

---

* "Deutero-Pauline" literally means written by a "second-Paul."

must be the main source of information about him, supplemented with data from Acts and indirect materials gleaned from the "deutero-Pauline" letters. What, then, do these sources tell us about this particular man?

For one thing, it is clear that Paul is proud of his heritage and upbringing, and the revealing passage, Phil. 3:5-6, tells much about his background. He writes that he was "circumcised on the eighth day, of the people of Israel, of the tribe of Benjamin, a Hebrew born of Hebrews; as to the Law a Pharisee, as to zeal a persecutor of the church, as to righteousness in the Law blameless."[37] (Most Bible quotes are from the Revised Standard Version.)

Additional biographical information is discernible in the letters. Paul seems to have suffered from some chronic physical disorder. He refers to this condition, for instance, as the reason for his stay in Galatia (Gal. 4:13-14). He seems to consider his illness as a sharing in the suffering of Jesus which has been given to him to constantly remind him that God's strength is most powerfully displayed through weakness (2 Cor. 12:7-10).[38]

In addition to this physical disorder, it seems likely that Paul was also not a very attractive or captivating public speaker. He imagines that the Corinthians make this assessment of him: "His letters are weighty and strong, but his bodily presence is weak, and his speech of no account" (2 Cor. 10:10). But even if he is "unskilled in speaking" (2 Cor. 11:6), he feels that Christ sent him to preach the gospel "and not with eloquent wisdom, lest the cross of Christ be emptied of its power" (1 Cor.1:17).

What Paul lacks in speaking skills he makes up for with his fiery personality. He is absolutely convinced that God has called him to spread the gospel to the Gentiles, and he tolerates no questioning of that commission, even from the other leaders of the "Jesus movement." "And from those who were reputed to be something (what they were makes no difference to me; God shows no partiality)—those, I say, who were of repute added nothing to me" (Gal. 2:6). Nor is Paul above tirades and angry outbursts against those he believes are spreading dangerous views. He claims that Peter has stood condemned for not being straightforward about the gospel (Gal. 2:11-14), he brands foes in Philippi as "dogs," "evil-workers," and "mutilators" (Phil. 3:2), and he wishes that his opponents in Galatia would literally castrate themselves (Gal. 5:12). Yet Paul is also capable of deep and moving prose. "I have been crucified with Christ; it is no longer I who live, but Christ who lives in me; and the life I now live in the flesh I live by faith in the Son of God, who loved me and gave himself for me" (Gal. 2:20).

It is also clear from the letters that Paul's career as an apostle of Jesus has not been without its hazards. He has been jailed, mocked, beaten, beset by dangers on the road, and ship-wrecked (2 Cor. 11:23-27).

Acts provides some further biographical details about Paul. He apparently was born in Tarsus, a major commercial center in Asia Minor (Acts 22:3), was therefore a citizen of the Roman Empire and entitled to certain privileges (22:25), and earned his living through the craft of tent-making (18:3).

This, then, is a preliminary background sketch of Paul—born and raised a Jew, also a Roman citizen, educated as a Pharisee, harasser of early Jesus believers, called by the Lord to bring the gospel to the Gentiles, a poor public speaker, afflicted with an unpleasant chronic condition, capable of explosive harshness, and also the writer of profound insights into the meaning of Jesus. It is to those insights that we shall now turn.

Questions for Reflection and Discussion

1. If the Bible is meant to be read in the context of the cultures of its writers, what dangers might there be in reading the scriptures "literally" without taking those cultural factors into account? Can you think of scriptural passages that have been the source of great controversy because they were understood "literally" and not "critically"?

2. Of what significance was the decision not to require circumcision for church membership?

3. From the comments about Paul in this introduction, what would make him appealing to you and what would turn you off?

4. What were some of the effects of the destruction of the Temple in Jerusalem?

5. Of what importance is the fact that the Jesus-movement was originally a grass-roots phenomenon?

CHAPTER TWO

Conversion or Call?

THE EVENT ITSELF

Our encounter with Paul begins with that event in which Paul experienced the presence of the Raised Jesus. As is well known, that experience had dramatic effects on Paul, most especially in that it transformed him from an opponent of the Jesus-movement to a missionary on its behalf. The precise nature of this transformation is what this chapter will explore.

It has been commonly presumed that Paul was moved by his experience of Christ to forsake his Jewish traditions and to "convert" to the newly founded Christianity. Such a view is related to the parallel assumption that Paul believed that the Torah had been terminated and replaced by Christ. (See Chapters 3 and 5.) This notion of Paul's abandonment of Judaism has been perpetuated by titling his encounter with Christ as "The Conversion of St. Paul." Now there is no doubt that Paul had to change his mind about some things because of experiencing Christ's presence. But the word *conversion*, when applied to Paul's experience, unavoidably carries the connotation of becoming a religious "convert," that is switching one's religious affiliation from one group to another.

There is growing evidence that thinking about Paul in such terms is inaccurate. For one thing, it has already been indicated (pages 12-13) that Christianity as a religion distinct from Judaism did not emerge until decades after Paul's death. How then can we talk as if Paul "converted" from one religion to another when the Jesus-movement of Paul's day was almost completely Jewish?

More importantly, how does Paul himself talk about his experience of Christ? Does he sound as if he had "converted" in the modern sense? Paul makes explicit reference to his encounter with the Raised Lord in Galatians 1:15-17:

> But when he who had set me apart before I was born, and had called me through his grace, was pleased to reveal his Son to me, in order that I might preach him among the Gentiles, I did not confer with flesh and blood, nor did I go up to Jerusalem to those who were apostles before me, but I went away into Arabia; and again I returned to Damascus.

It is notable that Paul refers to this revelation of the Lord in terms of a commission to "preach him among the Gentiles." In fact this account of Paul's experience occurs in the midst of passages in which Paul angrily asserts his authoritative appointment to spread the gospel to the Gentiles. For instance, "I laid before them the gospel...which I preach among the Gentiles" (Gal. 2:2); "I had been entrusted with the gospel to the uncircumcised" (2:7); and "he . . . worked through me also for the Gentiles"(2:8).

Paul's choice of words in describing his meeting with Christ also indicates that he thinks of the encounter in terms of a divine commissioning. Compare Paul's phrase in Gal 1:15, which literally rendered from the Greek reads, "set me apart from my mother's womb . . . that I might preach him among the nations" with the call of the prophet Isaiah in Is. 49:1, "The Lord called me from the womb," and in 49:6, "I will give you as a light to the nations that my salvation might reach to the ends of the earth." Jeremiah's calling also has a familiar ring, "Before I formed you in the womb I knew you, and . . . I appointed you a prophet to the nations" (Jer. 1:5).[1] Thus, Paul describes and understands his encounter with Jesus as a prophetic calling by God to preach the gospel to the Gentile nations.

The three accounts in Acts of Paul's "conversion" would also be more accurately described as Paul's calling. In all three Paul is commissioned to preach to the Gentiles: "He is a chosen instrument of mine to carry my name before the Gentiles . . ." (Acts 9:15); "I will send you far away to the Gentiles" (22:21); and most especially "But rise and stand upon your feet; for I have appeared to you for this purpose; to appoint you to serve and witness . . . [to] the Gentiles to whom I send you . . . "(26:16-17). The last citation is reminiscent of the call of the prophet Ezekiel: "Son of man, stand upon your feet . . . I am sending you . . . " (Ez. 2:1,3).[2]

If, then, we are to understand Paul's experience of Jesus as a prophetic call to be the "Apostle to the Gentiles,"[3] how does this call affect Paul's Jewishness? Does his divine commissioning alter his status as one "of the people of Israel, a Hebrew born of Hebrews . . . a Pharisee" (Phil. 3:5-6)?

AFTER THE EVENT: FAITHFUL JEW

Although, as shall be seen, Paul is absolutely convinced that Gentiles need not follow the Jewish Torah, he is also steeped in his rich Jewish heritage and believed that "the Torah was an expression of divine grace."[4] Some of Paul's reactionary enemies accused him of teaching Jews to cease Torah-observance, (Acts 21:21, "You have been teaching Jews to abandon the Law of Moses.") but nowhere does Paul state this in any of his letters.[5]

Indeed, the letters indicate the opposite viewpoint, namely that Jews were expected to continue living by the Torah even if they were in Christ. In 1 Cor. 7:17-18 Paul insists that everyone should remain as they were before they became a follower of Jesus; Jews should not seek to become Gentiles, and Gentiles should not seek to become Jews. Paul states in no uncertain terms, even though he is writing to Gentiles, that those who have been circumcised are "bound to keep the whole Law" (Gal. 5:3).

Furthermore, it seems that Paul himself remained a Torah-observant Jew throughout his lifetime. Such is the tradition Acts conveys. In Acts 16:3 Paul himself circumcises Timothy because his mother was Jewish, thereby making Timothy legally a Jew. Paul purifies himself in the Temple to demonstrate his faithfulness to the Torah in Acts 21:26, and while on trial Paul identifies his belief in resurrection as a Pharisaic teaching (23:6). But perhaps more significantly, Acts agrees with the evidence from Paul's own letters. For instance, could someone as faithful to Jewish traditions as James extend to Paul "the right hand of fellowship" (Gal. 2:9) knowing that Paul was an apostate Jew encouraging fellow Jews to also forsake their covenant commitment to the Torah? It would hardly seem possible.[6]

Thus, the description of Paul's dramatic encounter with Jesus as a "conversion" seems even more inappropriate. Both before and after the experience Paul remained a Torah-faithful Jew, but now one called by God to proclaim the gospel to the Gentiles.

BEFORE THE EVENT: PERSECUTOR

Therefore, how was Paul changed by his Jesus-event? As usual, Paul himself probably best describes the incident's effects. "I was still not known by sight to the churches of Christ in Judea; they only heard it said 'He who once persecuted us is now preaching the faith he once tried to destroy.' And they glorified God because of me" (Gal. 1:22-24). If the word "conversion" has any applicability to Paul, it would be to this abrupt reversal of a practice of "persecuting" the church.

Paul also refers to this past policy in 1 Cor. 15: 8-10: "Last of all, as to one untimely born, he appeared also to me. For I am the least of the apostles, unfit to be called an apostle, because I persecuted the church of God. But by the grace of God I am what I am, and his grace toward me has not been in vain." Paul does not give any reasons for his previous behavior other than to say he was extremely zealous for the traditions of his fathers (Gal. 1:14, see also Phil. 3:6).

According to the presupposition that Paul had "converted" from Judaism, it was generally supposed that Paul persecuted "Christians" because they no longer followed the Torah. After his "conversion" Paul supposedly saw the light and ceased to be Torah-observant himself. In fact there is some circumstantial support for this explanation in Acts' account of the death of Stephen. After giving a speech in which he denies any religious validity to the Temple (Acts 7:44-50) and in which he roundly condemns Judaism in general (7:35-53), Stephen has so enraged his Jewish listeners that they rise up and stone him to death. Acts depicts Paul as witnessing and consenting to this action (7:58, 8:1), then "ravaging the church by a house to house search" (8:3), and finally going to Damascus with orders from the High Priest to round up any "Christians" there (9:1-2). On the way Jesus appears to Paul and the "conversion" occurs. In this account, then, it appears that Paul is motivated to attack Jesus-followers because of their antipathy toward Judaism and its Torah, as exemplified by Stephen.

We have already seen that certain statements by Paul himself in his own letters conflict with this Acts account of his anti-church behavior. Recalling that Paul claimed he was "not known by sight to the churches of Christ in Judea" (Gal. 1:22), it seems unlikely that he was present at Stephen's death or that he persecuted the church in Jerusalem. Surely his victims would remember their oppressor's face, unless, of course, he wore a mask. Moreover, Damascus under Roman administration was far beyond the sphere of authority of the Judean High Priest. Paul receiving some sort of legal authorization from the High Priest in Jerusalem to go Christian-hunting in Damascus is quite impossible.[7]*

---

* It would be wise to recall the principle stated on pp. 15-16. When Acts and Paul are in disagreement, greater weight must be placed on Paul's own letters. His claim to be unknown in Judea must outweigh Acts' depictions of his persecuting activities. Acts is heavily influenced here by what is occurring while that book is being written. Its description of Paul's actions reflects the disputes between the church and the synagogue of the mid-80s when Acts was composed.

Most significantly, as has been indicated, Paul did not later teach that Jews should stop observing the Law. Nor did he believe, as Stephen apparently did, that the Law was useless. Directly contradicting such a notion Paul writes, "Do we then overthrow the Law by this faith? By no means! On the contrary, we uphold the Law" (Rom. 3:31).

Stephen's views, then, are not shared by Paul. As far as we can tell, many others did not accept Stephen's views. His fellow Hellenists disagreed with him,* although it seems that Hellenistic Jews in the church were identified with Stephen and had to flee the city. Moreover, the Jerusalem church continued to worship at the Temple regularly despite Stephen's attacks on it.[8]

The earlier explanation of Paul's persecution of the church, even though superficially substantiated by Acts, is not supported by the evidence from Paul's own letters. With the exception of the firebrand Stephen, the Jerusalem church *did* follow the Torah; Paul's own words make it very unlikely that he was on hand for Stephen's death, and Paul never changed his views about being a Torah-faithful Jew.

Why, then, did Paul persecute the church? If the issue was not whether Jews in the church should continue obeying the Torah, what was it? What would upset the "zealous" Pharisee Paul to the extent that he would take severe actions against the offenders? Whatever this thing was, Paul's views after encountering Christ were reversed.

Perhaps a clue can be found by noting that, as a believer in Jesus, Paul was absolutely adamant in insisting that through Christ God was calling Gentiles to be his people without having to "convert" to Judaism by being circumcised and following the Torah. (See for example, Gal. 3:14,26; 5:6.)

He defends this principle to the point of publicly castigating Peter's apparent vacillation on the point, as recounted in Gal. 2:11-14:

> But when Cephas [Peter] came to Antioch I opposed
> him to his face, because he stood condemned. For
> before certain men came from James, he ate with the

---

* Acts 6:9-11 indicates that he was opposed by members of a synagogue "from Cyrene and Alexandria."

Gentiles; but when they came he drew back and separated himself, fearing the circumcision party. And with him the rest of the Jews acted insincerely, so that even Barnabas was carried away by their insincerity. But when I saw that they were not straightforward about the truth of the gospel, I said to Cephas before them all, "If you, though a Jew, live like a Gentile and not like a Jew, how can you compel the Gentiles to live like Jews?"

Above all else, Paul desires to protect the right of Gentiles to be full members of the Jesus-movement on an equal basis with Jews.[9] By sharing table-fellowship, and probably the Lord's Supper as well, the Jews and Gentiles of the church in Antioch ritually demonstrated their equality before the God who had saved both groups. Apparently, Peter initially had no difficulty in eating with Gentiles, who, most likely being God-fearers, were probably observing some Jewish dietary customs anyway.* But seemingly out of fear of offending the newly-arrived Jews of the "circumcision party," Peter together with many Jews withdrew, leaving a divided community. It should be noted that the new arrivals must have advocated the position that Gentiles, even though Church members, should not be allowed into the table-fellowship of the church until they became Jews, a notion to which Paul is diametrically opposed. In any case, Paul cannot abide the division which results from Peter's actions and he forcefully condemns what he considers to be a betrayal of the gospel. What this incident reveals is that Paul's gospel, as will be made more evident in the next chapter, is essentially that God has called Gentiles to himself through Christ.[10]

This heart of Paul's gospel is undoubtedly what he realized as a result of his revelation of Jesus Christ. Before that experience Paul would not have acknowledged that God's righteousness could be revealed for the benefit of Gentiles in a new and startling way distinct from the revelation of the Torah. Logically, Paul, before his experience of the Raised Jesus, would oppose anyone who claimed that a person could become a child of God apart from the Torah.

---

* In Acts 15:20ff a letter is written to Gentiles which apparently codifies such minimal dietary observances.

This, therefore, explains Paul's persecution of the church. We have already seen that Hellenistic-Jewish members of the Jesus-movement had, at least in Antioch, begun to admit Gentiles to their ranks without requiring circumcision. Presumably, these Jewish members would associate freely with their Gentile brothers, and it would be this association that Paul would find most objectionable. He may have seen such fraternization as a threat to Jewish religious self-identity, and, being a Pharisee, Paul would be most interested in intensifying the Jewishness of his people, not in minimizing it.[11] The proximity of Antioch to Paul's native Tarsus combined with evidence that the earliest Hellenistic Jesus missionaries had travelled throughout the region (as stated in Acts 11: 19-20) makes it quite plausible that Paul would have encountered the first spreading of the Jesus-movement to Gentiles. Upon seeing Jews in close association with non-Torah-observant Gentiles, Paul would have been scandalized because he had not yet come to believe that through Christ God's call was extended even to the pagan Gentiles.[12] Paul then began bringing synagogue charges against the Jews involved, ultimately, perhaps, bearing witness against such Jews at the synagogue in Damsacus.[13]

This reconstruction would limit Paul's persecuting activities to the regions of Syria and Cilicia (in which Tarsus, Antioch, and Damascus are located), and would therefore explain why he was "not known by sight to the churches of Christ in Judea" (Gal 1:22). In this light it is very notable that shortly after his encounter with Christ, Paul "went into the regions of Syria and Cilicia" (Gal. 1:21), perhaps to undo the damage he had done. This would give even more meaning to the statement Paul quotes that "he who once persecuted us is now preaching the faith he once tried to destroy" (Gal. 1:23).

Paul always regarded his previous persecutions as his great sin[14]—he had failed to perceive that God was working through Christ on behalf of the Gentiles. Perhaps it is no coincidence that Paul's greatest criticism of his fellow Jews is that they have not seen that "the righteousness of God has been manifested apart from the Law" because God is God of the Gentiles as well as of the Jews (Rom. 3:21, 29). (This will be explored further in Chapter 3.) The great fault of his kinsmen was the same failure that Paul had been guilty of, and Paul was always amazed that in God's wisdom he had been chosen to undertake the very mission he had tried to thwart.

CONCLUSION

And so, it appears that before he encountered the Raised Jesus, Paul objected to and persecuted his fellow Jews who were entering into table-fellowship with Gentiles on the basis of their views about a Jesus whom they called Lord. Then Christ himself revealed the truth of the gospel to Paul, and appointed him Apostle to the Gentiles. Paul became convinced that it was God's will that Gentiles become part of his people without becoming Jews in the process. Paul immediately began to preach this astonishing news in the very regions in which he had been a persecutor. Throughout his career Paul continued to be Torah-observant.

Paul's unique experience of Jesus, therefore, should not be termed a "conversion" because of the associations that word has with changing religious affiliations. We have seen that Paul remained a Jew, but became a Jew with a divine mission to the Gentiles. Speaking of Paul's experience as a "call" is not only true to Paul's own description of it, but also emphasizes the main consequence of the encounter—Paul has been commissioned the herald to the Gentiles of the gospel of their salvation. The precise significance of this gospel will be examined in the following chapter.

Questions for Reflection and Discussion

1. How does the view of Paul's encounter with Jesus presented in this chapter differ from your previous ideas about it?

2. Paul and Stephen were both early followers of Jesus. How did their respective views about the Temple and Judaism seem to differ?

3. Speculate on reasons for Paul's anger about Peter's withdrawal from table-fellowship with Gentiles.

4. Paul's encounter with the Raised Jesus and his apostolic ministry to the Gentiles occurred before Christianity was a separate religion from Judaism. How does this affect your understanding of his experience as call?

5. What does this sentence mean to you?—"The Torah is an expression of divine grace."

CHAPTER THREE

Salvation for the Gentiles

THE CONVENTIONAL UNDERSTANDING

Many of the traditional assumptions about Paul are so inter-
related that changing any one of them immediately necessitates
alterations in the others. It has already been seen that in
presuming that Paul had converted away from Judaism, one
also had to assert that Paul believed the Law was no longer
to be followed. In this chapter further aspects of Paul's attitude
toward the Torah will be explored.

For centuries it has been commonly held that Paul came
to realize that trying to earn salvation by performing the works
required by the Law was futile because righteousness came only
through faith in Christ. This concept, known as justification
by faith, was considered to be the ultimate expression of Paul's
theology. It was understood that his previous life in Judaism
had been one of enslavement to the harsh strictures and

31

requirements of the Law, a joyless and somber existence. According to this line of thought, Paul eventually fought all who tried to subject Gentiles to the same legalistic captivity because "Christ redeemed us from the curse of the Law" (Gal. 3:13).[1]

In support of this traditional view, there are several passages in the letter to the Galatians in which Paul speaks in very harsh terms about the Law:

> O foolish Galatians!...Let me ask you only this: Did you receive the Spirit by works of the Law, or by hearing with faith? Are you so foolish?. . . .Does he who supplies the Spirit to you and works miracles among you do so by works of the Law or by faith? For all who rely on works of the Law are under a curse. . . .It is evident that no man is justified before God by the Law; for "He who through faith is righteous shall live." (Gal. 3:1,2,3,5,10,11.)

Note also his remarks that "if justification were through the Law, then Christ died to no purpose" (2:21); "the Law was our custodian until Christ came that we might be justified by faith" (3:24); and "Tell me, you who desire to be under law, do you not hear the Law? . . . We are not children of the slave but of the free woman. For freedom Christ has set us free; stand fast, therefore, and do not submit again to a yoke of slavery" (4:21,31-5:1).

Plainly, Paul is disputing unidentified opponents who are pressuring Gentiles to be circumcised and to live by Torah in order to deserve God's mercy. These opponents seem to believe that by following the Law one can earn the right to salvation. This is made clear by Paul's attacks on the idea throughout the letter, as in 2:16 for instance: "A man is not justified by works of the Law but through faith in Jesus Christ."

To Christian readers of later centuries the identity of Paul's foes seemed obvious. Surely Jews, with their scrupulous adherence to Torah dictates, believed that they were thereby earning their righteousness. Certainly those who "were confined under the Law . . . until Christ came" (Gal. 3:23-24) were the Jews. Paul's doctrine of justification by faith was thus understood to have grown out of his own experiences of the futility of Jewish legalities and his later joy in the faith of Christ. Now, it is certainly true that faith is extremely important for Paul. However, commentators have exalted Paul's statements regarding the necessity of faith by favorably contrasting them with an alleged works–righteousness assumed to be endemic to Judaism. Recent investigations into Jewish writings of the first and second centuries indicate that such an understanding of Judaism is not only completely false, but also that it greatly distorts Paul's profound message.

JUDAISM AND THE TORAH

Although the study of Jewish religious thought is a relatively new field for Christian theologians, it promises to have far-reaching implications.[2] Already it has necessitated a radical reassessment of our traditional understandings of Paul.

It is becoming undeniably clear that at the heart of Judaism is the awareness that God, in his unfathomable graciousness, had chosen Israel to be his people and had invited them into a covenantal pact with him. This "covenant was not earned, but . . . obedience to the commandments is the consequence of the prior election of Israel by God."[3] In other words, living a Torah-life was the only adequate response to having already been called into a saving relationship with God.[4] One sought to live by God's Way* and such seeking preserved one's covenantal status. Thus, the Judaism in which Paul was raised[5] appears to have been the exact opposite of the traditional Christian view of Judaism. Jews did not obey the Law in order to *become* saved; they followed the Law because that was what the God who had *already* chosen them wanted them to do!

It should also be observed that the rabbis did not teach that imperfect adherence to the Torah would cause someone to be damned. God's covenant was not thought to be dependent on obedience, but on the *intention* to be faithful to the covenant. Such intent would be expressed by doing one's best

---

* "Way" is probably a better translation of "Torah" than Law because it conveys the concept of it being a lifestyle much more fully than Law does. Law gives the impression that the Torah is just a set of rules.

to fulfill the commandments, and being repentant in times of error.[6] The rabbis held that "to be righteous was to be within the covenant despite one's failures."[7] Therefore, a Jew would not obey and repent in order to *earn* salvation, but to *maintain* his status as a member of the saved people.[8]

Moreover, Jews did not feel that Torah-observance was a form of slavery. It was, rather, their testimony to the God who had freed his people from bondage during the Exodus.[9] Since the Law was considered to be a gift from God, the revelation of how his people were to live, there was great joy in submitting to it.[10] Throughout Jewish history the Torah was conceived in terms of God's grace, God's gift of freedom.[11] Such conceptions are powerfully expressed in the Hebrew Scriptures. For example, consider these excerpts from Psalm 119, which seem as far removed as possible from any thought of slavery to the Law:

> Blessed are those whose way is blameless, who walk in the Law of the Lord! Blessed are those who keep his testimonies, who seek him with their whole heart, who also do no wrong, but walk in his ways!
>
> With my whole heart I will seek thee; let me not wander from thy commandments! Blessed be thou, O Lord; teach me thy statutes! With my lips I will declare the ordinances of thy mouth. In the way of thy testimonies I delight as much as in all riches. I will meditate on they precepts, and fix my eyes on thy ways. I will delight in thy statutes; I will not forget thy word.
>
> Open my eyes, that I may behold wondrous things out of thy Law. I am a sojourner on earth; hide not thy commandments from me! My soul is consumed with longing for thy ordinances at all times. Thy testimonies are my delight, they are my counselors.
>
> Put false ways far from me; and graciously teach me thy Law! I have chosen the way of faithfulness, I set thy ordinances before me. I will run in the way of thy commandments when thou enlargest my understanding! Give me understanding that I may keep thy Law and observe it with my whole heart. Lead me

in the path of thy commandments, for I delight in it. Behold, I long for thy precepts; in thy righteousness give me life! Let thy steadfast love come to me, O Lord, thy salvation according to thy promise.

I will keep thy Law continually and for ever and ever; and I shall walk at liberty, for I have sought thy precepts (Psalm 119: 1-3,10,12-16,18-20,24, 29-30, 32,34-35,40-41,44-45).

This psalm, together with a wide range of Jewish literature, makes it plain that the election of Israel and its ultimate salvation "are considered to be the result of God's mercy rather than human achievement."[12] In short, Jews did not try to "earn" salvation. To use Pauline terminology, one might say that Jews were justified by their faith-relationship with the One who had given them the Law.

A careful reading of Paul, without the conventional stereotyped understanding of Judaism, shows that Paul the Pharisee never claimed that Jews thought they could earn God's favor. He not only quotes the Hebrew scriptures to prove the opposite (as in Gal. 3:11 where Paul cites Hab. 2:4, "he who through faith is righteous shall live"), but he also states that "we ourselves, who are Jews by birth and not Gentile sinners . . . know that a man is not justified by works of the Law" (Gal.2:16-17. The rest of verse 17 and "faith in Christ" will be discussed in Chapter 5.) This verse gives some indication of the identity of Paul's Galatian opponents. If Judaism did not subscribe to a theology of righteousness based on works, then who were these opponents who did?

PAUL'S GALATIAN OPPONENTS

To ascertain the identity of Paul's foes in Galatia, it might be well to list some of the conclusions reached thus far:

1. Paul is convinced of a divine call to bring Gentiles into the church.
2. He is adamant that simply by faith in the Lordship of Jesus, Gentiles may be baptized and admitted. They do not have to become Jews by being circumcised and

following the Torah.

3. His opponents are urging Gentiles to be circumcised in order to merit their salvation by works of the Law.
4. "Jews from birth" did not believe that by following the Torah they earned salvation.

It would seem, however, that the opponents believed that Jews followed the Torah to earn salvation, even though Jews themselves had no such notion. Recalling that there were Gentiles who had become attracted by Judaism to the point of observing some Torah regulations, it becomes apparent that Paul's Galatian opponents are actually Judaism-infatuated Gentiles![13] Perhaps these opponents have gone so far as to become circumcised themselves (thereby becoming proselytes) but they have done so with erroneous views of Judaism. They do not believe Paul's assertions that the faith of Christ is sufficient to account them righteous. Rather, they are pressuring their Gentile brethren to cover all their bases, so to speak, by being circumcised in order to guarantee their salvation.

There are several passages in Galatians which confirm the non-Jewish identity of the opponents. "For even those who receive circumcision do not themselves keep the Law, but they desire to have you circumcised that they may glory in your flesh," (6:13) glory in the power over you they would thereby demonstrate. Also "all who rely on works of the Law are under a curse; for it is written 'Cursed be everyone who does not abide by all the things written in the book of the Law and do them' " (3:10). By thus quoting Deuteronomy 27:26, Paul uses the Law itself to demonstrate that a superficial, hocus-pocus attitude toward the Torah is condemnable. The opponents are not really interested in becoming partners in the Jewish covenant; they only want to observe a shallow, magic-like ritual to bolster their own weak faith. Such an attitude is directly opposed to the gospel of Paul because, "You are severed from Christ, you who would be justified by the Law; you have fallen away from grace" (5:4). By acting out of a superstitious belief in works-righteousness, the opponents are presuming that they can earn their own way to salvation and are thereby not accepting God's free gift (or grace) of righteousness through Christ. Indeed, by receiving circumcision with such a hocus-pocus mentality, "Christ will be of no advantage" (5:2). "Whoever those Jew-mimicking Gentiles were with whom Paul had to contend, they clearly had distorted the witness of Judaism,"[14] and had forsaken Paul's gospel as well.

GENTILES UNDER THE LAW

Since Paul considers himself to be the Apostle to the Gentiles, since the Galatian church is a Gentile community, and since his opponents are Gentiles with perverted views of Judaism, it seems plain that the problems Paul addresses in the letter to the Galatians are Gentile issues and not Jewish ones at all. Given these factors, and noting the frequent references to "the law" in the letter, it is interesting that only in recent times has the question been raised of how Jews considered the Torah to affect Gentiles.[15]

This question can be approached by focusing our attention on Paul's phrase "under the law," and by asking who are the people being so described. Admittedly, it is difficult to arrive at a precise identification because Paul uses the word "law" in different senses.[16] Among other things, it can refer to a law of the flesh, the sinful state of the corrupt world, which is a frequent usage in the letter to the Romans: "But I see in my members another law at war with the law of my mind and making me captive to the law of sin which dwells in my members" (Romans 7:23). As we have seen, "law" can also be *the* Law, the Jewish Torah as in Romans 7:12: "So the Law is holy, and the commandment is holy and just and good."

The phrase "under the law" can have similar but different usages as is plain in Galatians 4:4 where Paul notes that "when the time had fully come, God sent forth his Son born of woman, born under the law, to redeem those who were under the Law,* so that we might receive adoption as sons." Paul is arguing that Christ became a human being, subject to all the sinfulness of fleshy existence,[17] in order to save those who by Torah standards were not sons of God.

Our interest here is in the identity of those whom Paul

---

* To indicate these differing senses, *law* has been left in small letters when referring to the law of a sinful world, and capitalized to *Law* when speaking about the Torah.

says are "under the Law" (in the sense of the Torah). Traditionally, it has been assumed that they were Jews. The observation that Paul is almost always addressing and concerned with Gentiles should caution against making that assumption too hastily. There are other contrary signs as well.

First, it should be noted that Paul always uses the term in a negative way; being "under the Law" is not a desirable state of affairs. For instance Galatians 3:10, "All who rely on works of the Law are *under* a curse;" or 3:23, "Now before faith came we were confined under the Law, kept under restraint until faith should be revealed;" or 4:5, Christ came "to redeem those under the Law."

Now we have seen (p. 34) that Jews did not consider submission to the Law to be something dreadful, rather it was a joyous opportunity! The phrase "under the Law" is found in no Jewish literature to connote the Torah-covenant,[18] and, in fact, since the expression seems to indicate being under the *curse* of the Law, it is a phrase no Jew (including Paul) could use to describe Israel's relationship to the Torah.[19]

Furthermore, Paul himself seems to have other people than Jews in mind when he uses the expression. In 1 Cor. 9:19-23 Paul enunciates one of his policies while he preaches the gospel; he adapts his words and manners to his particular audience:

> For though I am free from all men, I have made myself a slave to all, that I might win the more. To the Jews I became as a Jew, in order to win Jews. To those under the Law I became as one under the Law—though not being myself under the Law—that I might win those under the Law. To those outside the Law I became as one outside the Law—not being without Law toward God but under the Law of Christ—that I might win those outside the Law. To the weak I became weak, that I might win the weak. I have become all things to all men, that I might by all means save some. I do it for the sake of the gospel, that I may share in its blessings.

What is noteworthy here is Paul's discussion of four distinct groups: (1)Jews, (2)those under the Law, (3)the lawless (those

Corinthians who feel themselves beyond any law whatsoever), and (4)the weak (those whose faith is easily shaken as discussed in 1 Cor. 8-10).[20] Of special importance is his categorization of Jews and those under the Law as two distinct groups! Those under the Law, those somehow accursed by it (a group from which Paul excludes himself in vs. 20) are Gentiles!

We come back, then, to a question posed earlier. How are Gentiles under the Law's curse? How did the Torah affect Gentiles?

Recent investigations are revealing that some Jews in Paul's time believed that God, in the distant past, had offered all the nations the chance to live by his Way, by his Torah. All the nations but Israel refused, finding one commandment or another to be too restrictive. Thus the Gentile nations came under the Law's curse because "they are without excuse" (Rom. 1:20) for not heeding God's Way. They had refused out of their own selfishness.[21] As an example of this strain of Jewish thought, 4 Ezra 7:20-24, written before the end of the first century, asserts:[22]

> Let many perish who are now living, rather than the Law of God which is set before them be disregarded! For God strictly commanded those who came into the world, when they came, what they should do to live, and what they observe to avoid punishment. Nevertheless they were not obedient, and spoke against him; they devised for themselves vain thoughts, and proposed to themselves wicked frauds; they even declared that the Most High does not exist, and they ignored his ways! They scorned his Law, and denied his decrees; they have been unfaithful to his statutes, and have not performed his works.

If Paul, as Rom. 1:20 makes likely, held some such views, then the Galatian situation would be for him even more pathetic. No hope was open to the Galatian Gentiles by way of the Law which their fathers had rejected.[23] Their only means of salvation was the new revelation of God's mercy through Jesus Christ. Poignantly, the Gentiles for whom Paul felt responsible were demonstrating the shallowness of their faith by readily accepting superstitious, works-righteousness propaganda.

Did Paul believe that Gentiles were under the curse of the Law? It seems very likely. While addressing Gentiles, not only does he constantly speak of Christ as freeing those under the Law's curse, but he also makes a relevant reference in Gal. 3:19 when he argues that the Law was "ordained by angels through an intermediary." There is no Jewish notion of the Torah having been given to Israel by angels. Rather, this passage seems to refer to the Jewish conception that seventy angels oppressively ruled the Gentile nations by using the Torah to point out all of their pagan sinfulness.[24] Thus once more we see Paul well-versed in contemporary Jewish thought, asserting the condemnatory nature of the Torah upon Gentiles.

Following the principle stated in 1 Cor. 9:20-21, Paul often includes himself with the Galatian Gentiles by using the familiar, first person plural "we," (as in Gal. 3:23, "we were confined under the Law"). But he is clearly addressing a purely Gentile dilemma—how to escape from the curse of the Jewish God's Law. If such a worry was prevalent among Gentile God-fearers, then their readiness to accept circumcision to avoid God's curse is understandable.

As Apostle to the Gentiles, Paul feels obligated to save the nations from the Law's condemnation. In Galatia, that mission was being threatened by proselytes with magical notions about the Law who were shaking the young church's new-found faith and hope in Christ. And that faith, according to Paul, was the only way for Gentiles to become righteous before God.

CHRIST AND THE PROMISES TO ABRAHAM

The very possibility that Gentiles at large could become righteous is a wonderful development for Paul. Through faith Gentiles as well as Jews can be accounted God's children. In Gal. 4:4-7, Paul asserts that at the proper moment God sent his Son so that Gentiles "might receive adoption as sons." As sons, Gentiles can now call God "Abba! Father!" and are no longer slaves but heirs. This divine adoption is, for Paul, the culmination of God's grand design for humanity—that design which was first revealed to Abraham. "In Christ Jesus the blessing of Abraham might come upon the Gentiles" (Gal. 3:14) for "if you are Christ's then you are Abraham's offspring, heirs according to promise" (3:29).

The Gentiles, then, can now become God's children, a status that previously was restricted to Jews in the Covenant of Abraham. But now, Paul believes, God's mercy and graciousness has "been manifested apart from the Law" (Romans 3:21). God has confirmed his promise to Abraham that he would be "the father of many nations" (a promise recounted in Gen. 17:4-6,16, and quoted by Paul in Rom. 4:17ff) by now including Gentiles as his heirs. The scriptural promise that Israel would be a light to the nations and that the nations would say, "Come, let us go up to the mountain of the Lord, to the house of the God of Jacob, that he may teach us his ways and we may walk in his paths" (Micah 4:2) had now been fulfilled in Jesus![25]

Paul carries this logic further in Gal. 4:21-31 where he warns the Galatians not to become a children of slavery like Abraham's son Ishmael (son of Abraham's slave Hagar). In rabbinic thought, Ishmael boasted that he was more righteous than Isaac because he had freely chosen to be circumcised at the age of thirteen. Isaac was circumcised as an infant, and so, according to Ishmael, had no conscious commitment to God. This boasting about circumcision neatly parallels the thoughts of Paul's Galatian opponents. Paul urges his readers not to be Ishmaels, children of slavery, who boast in the flesh. Instead they should be like Isaac, child of the promise, who was born according to God's Spirit in response to faith. The Galatians, now in Christ heirs to Abraham's promise, must be heirs to Abraham's faith also. They should not be trying to do things to merit God's favor, but should accept his generosity as an undeserved gift.[26]

Paul's conceptions about what God has done through Christ for the Gentiles seem to have been wonderfully preserved by the writer of the letter to the Ephesians. In Eph. 2:11-3:6, this follower of Paul speaks to Gentiles in the church about the hostility which had previously existed between Jews and Gentiles. Writing in Paul's name, he instructs that Jesus did away with the Law which condemned Gentiles. By his death, Jesus brought Jews and Gentiles together as fellow recipients of God's mercy. The writer builds up to an exciting punch line when he states that God's secret plan, which had been hidden for ages, has now been revealed to Paul. That secret mystery is that through Christ Gentiles have now been made co-heirs with Jews, fellow partakers of the promise in Christ (3:6).

Because of what God has done in Christ, Gentiles can now become "honorary Jews,"[27] so to speak. They do not become members of the Covenant of Abraham but they benefit from the fruition of its promises. By faith they too become God's children, and in response must live by the Way of Christ. (Just as Jews in response to their election must live by the Way of Torah!) How Gentiles in Christ should conduct themselves will be explored in the next chapter.

CONCLUSION

Although Paul teaches that justification is by faith, he clearly does not mean that as some sort of criticism of Judaism (as has been popularly supposed). Instead, he invites Gentiles to enter into a faith-relationship with God through Christ. Such a faith not only saves Gentiles from the curse of the Jewish Law, but it also makes them sisters and brothers of Jews by adoption.

It might be more accurate, then, to say that through faith salvation is possible for all. Through faith in their election, Jews live God's way of the Torah. Through faith in their calling by Jesus, which confirms Torah promises, Gentiles live God's Way as embodied in Jesus. It is the fact that salvation is freely available to all that inspires Paul to speak of justification by faith. That Gentiles can now be saved is the best expression of Paul's message. The ramifications of that message will be the subject of the next two chapters.

Questions for Reflection and Discussion

1. If, as Paul believes, one is accounted righteous before God because of one's faith, how might this principle be applied today to Jews living in the Torah-covenant?

2. As a Christian living today, what effect does the concept of Gentiles becoming "honorary Jews" have on the understanding of your faith?

3. How does Paul's thinking about Torah as Israel's grateful response to God's gift of election relate to modern differences between Jewish and Christian religious beliefs?

4. How might you describe the stereotyped Gentile understanding of Judaism? What is its source?

5. To what extent did Paul draw from his rabbinic knowledge in teaching Gentiles the Good News about salvation in Christ?

CHAPTER FOUR

Gentiles in Christ

AN INCONSISTENT PAUL

When one believes that Paul had thrown off the legalistic shackles of the hated Law and had entered into the freedom of Christ, it is quite difficult to explain such Pauline remarks as:

> If we live by the Spirit, let us also walk by the Spirit. Let us have no self-conceit, no provoking of one another, no envy of one another. Brethren, if a man is overtaken in any trespass, you who are spiritual should restore him in a spirit of gentleness. Look to yourself, lest you too be tempted. Bear one another's burdens, and so fulfill the Law of Christ (Gal. 5:25-6:2).

> For neither circumcision counts for anything nor uncircumcision, but keeping the commandments of God (1 Cor. 7:19).

45

Owe no one anything, except to love one another; for he who loves his neighbor has fulfilled the Law. The commandments, "You shall not commit adultery, You shall not kill, You shall not steal, You shall not covet," and any other commandment, are summed up in this sentence, "You shall love your neighbor as yourself." Love does no wrong to a neighbor; therefore love is the fulfilling of the Law (Romans 13: 8-10).

It seems plain that Paul is urging his readers to follow what he calls the "Law of Christ," which apparently incorporates many commandments from the Torah. How could one who had supposedly boasted about his freedom from the Law advocate submission to some new legal system?[1]

Based on the perspectives presented in previous chapters, there is substantial evidence that this apparent Pauline inconsistency is the result of the modern reader's mistaken assumptions about the authenticity of Paul's Jewishness. We have attempted in earlier chapters to demonstrate that Paul never thought himself free from the gift of living according to the Torah. Nor did he encourage his Jewish brethren to cease Torah-life, even when they had come to acknowledge Jesus as Lord. His main concern was to save Gentiles from certain condemnation by making them "honorary Jews,"[2] heirs to the promises of universal salvation given to Abraham.

This perspective leads to a resolution of Paul's supposed inconsistency in his thoughts about "law." We shall see that Paul's "Law of Christ," or its alternate expression to "live by the Spirit," is in many respects an extension to Gentiles of various Jewish ethical, moral, and theological principles.[3]

Being "In Christ"

Paul uses some unique phrases and terms to convey his deep theological insights. The expression "in Christ," for instance, is often used to connote membership in the church: "To the church of God which is at Corinth, to those sanctified in Christ Jesus ..." (1 Cor.1:2); "To all the saints in Christ Jesus who are at Philippi ..."(Phil.1:1); "For as many of you as were baptized into Christ have put on Christ ... for you are all one in Christ Jesus" (Gal. 3:27,28); and "Do you not know that all of us who have been baptized into Christ Jesus were baptized into his death?" (Romans 6:3).

Paul seems to understand the church to be the abiding presence of Christ in the world. It is through the community of Jesus that the Raised Lord is manifested to humanity.[4] He also uses another of his original phrases to make this point to the church at Corinth: "By one Spirit we were all baptized into one body ... you are the body of Christ and individually are members of it" (1 Cor. 12:13,27).

Through baptism the person of faith becomes part of Christ. The life of the Raised Lord is made available to members of the community of the church, members who are gradually "being transformed into his likeness" by his Spirit (2 Cor. 3:18).[5] Clearly, Paul is expressing the idea that by being part of the church, one is a member of a saved community which will ultimately share in the resurrection of its Lord (note also 2 Cor.4:14, "He who raised the Lord Jesus will raise us also"; 1 Cor. 15:22, "In Christ shall all be made alive"; Romans 6:5, "We shall certainly be united with him in a resurrection like his"; and 1 Thes. 4:17, "We ... shall be caught up together ... with the Lord").

To be outside of this saved community is to be subject to the evils of the external world. That is the underlying concept behind 1 Cor. 5:1-5. In these verses Paul expresses both his shock that a member of the church is living in incest and his utter astonishment that the Corinthians have the arrogance to brag about this person. Paul's corrective is notable: "Let him who has done this thing be removed from among you. . . . You are to deliver this man to Satan for the destruction of the flesh, that his spirit may be saved in the day of the Lord Jesus" (5:2b,5). It is Paul's hope that once thrust from the community of the saints, the offender will be shocked back to his senses by being directly exposed to the world's evil influences.[6] However, in the saved community "the Spirit of him who raised Christ Jesus from the dead will give life to your mortal bodies also through his Spirit which dwells in you" (Romans 8:11).

This preaching of Paul that entry into Christ brings one

into a community of salvation parallels Jewish thought regarding the Election of Israel. By choosing Israel as his people and giving her the Torah-covenant, God has promised all Israel a share in the world to come. "All who are maintained in the covenant by obedience, atonement, and God's mercy belong to the group which will be saved."[7] By living according to the Torah, faithful Jews witness to their membership in the saved community of God's Chosen People.

Paul apparently applies the same concept to the new community which is open to Gentiles. By being part of the "new covenant" of Christ's death and rising (1 Cor. 11:25), followers of Jesus are also in a saved community of God's people.[8] Does it not logically follow that those brought into salvation through Christ must live by some "Law of Christ," just as Jews in their covenant abide by the Torah?

LIFE IN SIN VS. LIFE IN CHRIST (OR IN CHRIST'S SPIRIT)

In several of his letters Paul provides lists which contrast life in Christ's Spirit to life in sin:

> And since they did not see fit to acknowledge God, God gave them up to a base mind and improper conduct. They were filled with all manner of wickedness, evil, covetousness, malice. Full of envy, murder, strife, deceit, malignity, they are gossips, slanderers, haters of God, insolent, haughty, boastful, inventors of evil, disobedient to parents, foolish, faithless, heartless, ruthless (Rom. 1:28-31).

> Let us conduct ourselves becomingly as in the day, not in reveling and drunkenness, not in debauchery and in licentiousness, not in quarreling and jealousy (Rom. 13:13).

> I wrote to you in my letter not to associate with immoral men; not at all meaning the immoral of this world, or the greedy and robbers, or idolaters, since then you would need to go out of the world. But rather I wrote to you not to associate with anyone who bears the name of brother if he is guilty of immorality or greed, or is an idolater, reviler, drunkard,

or robber—not even to eat with such a one (1 Cor. 5:9-11).

Do you not know that the unrighteous will not inherit the kingdom of God? Do not be deceived; neither the immoral, nor idolaters, nor adulterers, nor sexual perverts, nor thieves, nor the greedy, nor drunkards, nor revilers, nor robbers will inherit the kingdom of God. And such were some of you (1 Cor. 6:9-11a).

For I fear that perhaps I may come and find you not what I wish; that perhaps there may be quarreling, jealousy, anger, selfishness, slander, gossip, conceit, and disorder. I fear that when I come again my God may humble me before you, and I may have to mourn over many of those who sinned before and have not repented of the impurity, immorality, and licentiousness which they have practiced (2 Cor. 12: 20-21).

Now the works of the flesh are plain: fornication, impurity, licentiousness, idolatry, sorcery, enmity, strife, jealousy, anger, selfishness, dissension, party spirit, envy, drunkenness, carousing, and the like. I warn you as I warned you before, that those who do such things shall not inherit the kingdom of God (Gal.5: 19-21).

It is interesting to note that these forbidden actions are also prohibited to those who live by Torah, as this summary chart indicates:

COMMUNITY STRIFE	Lev. 19:17-18. Deut. 22:1-4.
COVETOUSNESS	Ex. 20:17. Deut. 5:21.
DECEIT, SLANDER	Ex. 20:16. Lev. 19:11. Deut. 5:20; 19:16-20.
DISOBEDIENCE TO PARENTS	Ex. 20:12. Lev. 19:3; 20:9. Deut. 5:16; 21:18-21; 27:16.
PRIDE, CONCEIT	Deut. 8: 17-18; 9: 4,6.
SELFISHNESS, GREED	Deut. 15:11.
SEXUAL MISCONDUCT	Ex. 20:14. Lev. 18:1-30; 20:10-21. Deut. 5:18; 22:22-30; 27:20.

Most of the items on Paul's lists of sinful behavior can also be seen to fall into two broad categories. Those offenses affecting harmonious community life (quarreling, gossip, disorder, dissension, party spirit, faithlessness, heartlessness, ruthlessness, enmity, jealousy, strife, envy, malice) and those involving sexual misconduct (immorality, perversion, adultery, carousing, licentiousness, debauchery) are given the most attention in the Pauline lists.

It seems reasonable to conclude that sexual misconduct concerns Paul so much, at least partially, because of his Jewish heritage. Note in the chart how frequently the Torah addresses the topic. The other major topic, community life, is emphasized because of Paul's views on how the church should function, as will be seen.

Now this parallelism between Pauline and Torah definitions of sin is not conclusive proof that Paul is extending to Gentiles Jewish moral principles. Similar lists of improper ethical behavior were widespread in the Greek world from non-Jewish sources.[9] Noteworthy, however, is another practice Paul attributes to Gentiles which appears in four of the lists quoted above—not acknowledging God as the One or idolatry. It would seem from Romans 1:28-31 that Paul believes all the other sins occurred because "they did not see fit to acknowledge God."*

In Judaism the crime of turning to other gods is the utmost betrayal of the Covenant, violating the essential Judaic principle: "Hear, O Israel—the Lord our God is one Lord" (Deut. 6:4). The concern for loyalty to the One alone is obvious from a quick reading through Deuteronomy and Leviticus where injunctions against idolatry appear dozens of times.**

This deep and widespread Jewish abhorrence for idolatry is reflected in Paul's frequent attacks upon it, and clearly shows his rootedness in Jewish norms. He desires Gen-

---

* Paul attacks the worship of idols often. Besides the four references cited on pp. 48-49, see also 1 Cor. 10:7,14,19-21; 12:2. 2 Cor. 6:16. 1 Thess. 1:9.

** See Lev. 19:4,26,31; 20:6,27; 26:1-2. Deut. 5:6-10; 6:4-5,13,14; 7:4,25; 8:19; 12:2-3; 13:1-18; 17:2-5; 18:9-14; 27:15; 30:17-18. Some of these condemn sorcerers & wizards—those who consort with foreign gods. (Note, too, Gal. 5:20 where idolatry is followed by sorcery.)

tiles to live righteous lives, and that righteousness is defined by Jewish ethical principles.

It should be noted, though, that Paul's encouragement of a "Jewish" lifestyle does not include Jewish Sabbath or cultic or dietary regulations.[10] For instance, he agrees that those in Christ should feel free to eat meat which had been offered to idols because such idols have no real existence (1 Cor. 8:4-6). Paul does not believe that Gentiles in Christ should become Jews by observing the whole Torah, but they must live by God's commands of morality. Such commands, Paul suggests, are "fulfilled in one word, 'You shall love your neighbor as yourself' " (Gal. 5:14, quoting Lev. 19:18). The ethical commandment to love one's neighbor is also present in the discussion about idol-meat just cited. Although those in Christ *can* eat meat offered to idols, they *should not* if such an action would confuse and scandalize their brothers (1 Cor. 8: 7-13). Concern for neighbor motivates Paul's closing sentence about the subject: "If food is the cause of my brother's falling, I will never eat meat, lest I cause my brother to fall" (8:13).

And so, all of the sins and evils listed previously are to be countered by authentic, heart-felt love:

> Let love be genuine; hate what is evil, hold fast to what is good; love one another with brotherly affection; outdo one another in showing honor. Never flag in zeal, be aglow with the Spirit, serve the Lord. Rejoice in your hope, be patient in tribulation, be constant in prayer. Contribute to the needs of the saints, practice hospitality. Bless those who persecute you; bless and do not curse them. Rejoice with those who rejoice, weep with those who weep. Live in harmony with one another; do not be haughty, but associate with the lowly; never be conceited. Repay no one evil for evil, but take thought for what is noble in the sight of all. If possible, so far as it depends upon you, live peaceably with all. Do not be overcome by evil, overcome evil with good. (Rom. 12:9-18,21)

Such a lifestyle, the life of "the Lord who is the Spirit" (2 Cor. 3:18), results in the fruits of that Spirit "love, joy, peace, patience, kindness, goodness, gentleness, self-control" (Gal.5:22-23)—the very opposites of the life of sin.

The love-command, which encapsulizes life in the Spirit of Christ, is used by Paul to correct basic social evils in the church at Corinth. Corinthian factionalism, eucharistic disorders, envy of spiritual gifts, and boasting are all addressed by Paul's famous words about love in 1 Cor. 13:13,"the greatest [of all virtues] is love."

How are Paul's Gentile readers to come to live this life in the Spirit? It is notable that Paul does not urge on Gentiles the life based on love because such a life is prescribed by the Torah (although Paul himself described that life with the Torah in mind). Rather, he points to Christ as the model of the life his followers should lead. With his characteristic self-confidence Paul instructs, "Be imitators of me, as I am of Christ" (1 Cor. 11:1).* For Paul, Christ is the vehicle of the Gentiles' salvation. He is the ultimate criterion of goodness.[11]

CHRIST: THE TRUE MAN (ADAM)

Why is Christ so important for Paul? What about him makes him so significant? What did Jesus do that makes the salvation of God universal in scope?

Such questions can be answered by exploring Paul's references to Christ as "the New Adam" or "the New Man." This image is not only very profound, it may also be an original Pauline contribution to early church christological** reflection.[12]

To see the expression in all of its implications, it is necessary to point out that the Genesis creation accounts explicitly assert that the first Adam (the first Man) was made in the image or likeness of God.*** Because of the Man's fall, sin and death enter into creation.

---

* See also 1 Cor. 4:16, "I urge you, then, be imitators of me;" and 1 Thess. 1:6, "You became imitators of us. . . ."

** Christology is the branch of religious thought which considers the meaning, nature, and significance of Christ for the world. In New Testament times there were several christologies, or ways of thinking about Christ, present. This section examines Paul's christology.

*** See Genesis 1:26-27; 5:1-3; 9:6.

Recalling Paul's lists of sins from the previous section, sin could be generally defined as a grasping, self-centered egocentrism. Sin is ultimately the acting out of pure self-interest without regard for anyone else. Paul feels that it was this egocentric lifestyle that the Man introduced into the world, and it has prospered and spread ever since. "Therefore, as sin came into the world through one man and death through sin, so death spread to all men because all men sinned" (Rom. 5:12).

It should be observed that this self-centered or sinful way of life is the opposite of the way Jews believe God operates. Above all things God is a God of generosity, graciousness, and love. He created the world out of love and made human beings "in his image" so that they could be loving, caring co-creators of the world.[13]* To the extent, then, that people sin (or are egocentric), they are not in the image of the loving, other-centered, creating God. They are not being human as God intended and designed them to be human.

Paul, however, says that Christ "is the likeness (image) of God" (2 Cor. 4:4). Referring back to the Genesis creation accounts, Paul goes on to say that "it is the God who said, 'let light shine out of darkness' who has shone in our hearts to give the light of knowledge of the glory of God in the face of Christ" (4:6).

This is why Jesus is the New Adam or the New Man. He is human the way God always intended people to be human—by being in God's image. Those who join Paul in imitating Christ "are being changed into his likeness from one degree of glory to another" (2 Cor. 3:18).

This is also why Paul so often refers to Christ's death. Being willing to die for others is the ultimate sign of being in God's other-centered image. Thus, "God shows his love for us in that while we were yet sinners Christ died for us" (Rom. 5:8) and "I have been crucified with Christ; it is no longer I who live, but Christ who lives in me; and the life I now live in the flesh I live by faith in the Son of God, who loved me and gave himself for me" (Gal. 2:20).

Adam's "trespass which led to condemnation for all

---

* This theme of the loving nature of God is common. Note, for example, Deut. 7:7, the Lord chose Israel "because the Lord loves you."

men," is corrected by Jesus' self-giving death, an "act of righteousness which leads to acquittal and life for all men" (Rom. 5:18). Those who have been baptized into Christ's death (Rom.6:3) have crucified their old sinful lifestyle (6:6, see also Gal. 5:24), and now "walk in the newness of life" (Rom. 6:4)— the life which Christ lived in God's image.

Christ has demonstrated that it is possible to live the loving, caring humanity in God's image. Therefore, sin, while still in existence, should have no power over those living the life of Christ (the theme of Chapter 6 of Romans). The church is to be the community of believers living in Christ's/God's image. They live a lifestyle of authentic, God-intended humanity rooted in love. This church, therefore, rejects the distorted, self-centered value system permeating the outside world.[14] With this concept of church in mind, it is no wonder that Paul is so upset and exasperated by the doings in Corinth. Rather than living in Christ, they are displaying the characteristics of the sinful world!

All of these ideas about Christ as the New Man living in God's image might be usefully presented in graphic form:

GOD
Whose love is so great it calls
all creation into being. God's
creative love makes humanity
"in his image."

HUMANITY IN GOD'S IMAGE
is meant to be loving, empowering, concerned with
others. Humanity is graced with free-will to freely
choose this God-like lifestyle.

↓   ↓

(continued on p. 55)

DISTORTED OR SINFUL
HUMANITY
chosen by the Man is a
false, unGodlike lifestyle
based on selfishness or egocentrism. This distortion of
God's intentions pervades
human society with a false,
distorted value system and
exerts a corrosive, unGodly
effect on all humanity.

CHRIST
lived a human life which
was truly "in God's image."
By loving and cherishing
others he enabled them to
choose to be Godlike themselves. His willingness to
die for others was the ultimate expression of a human
life he lived in the image of
God.

THE CHURCH,
the community of Jesus' followers, is committed to living, like Christ, in a loving,
enabling, freeing fellow-
ship. Baptism brings people
into a sharing in Christ's
death—they die to sin's
dominance. They also
come to share in his life, the
life of humanity in God's
image.

LIFE IN THE FLESH,
the continuing effects of
sin, foster a self-centered,
unGodlike way of life
which ends only in death.

How many of these profound insights are rooted in Paul's Jewish heritage?

The idea of Adam as representative of all humanity is present in Jewish writings around Paul's time. He is used as a symbol of the unity of humankind which had been subsequently shattered, but which will one day be restored. It is probable that Paul was familiar with these thoughts and saw them useful in his reflections about Christ.[15]

Also, it was (and is) a Jewish insight that Creation was incomplete and awaited the ultimate fulfillment of God's designs for it.[16] Paul, the Jew who held Jesus as Lord, believed that in Christ God had begun this New Creation. The prototype of real humanity in God's image had appeared and all humanity was being conformed to him. "If anyone is in Christ he is a new creation; the old has passed away, behold, the new has come" (2 Cor. 5:17). Furthermore, all "creation waits with eager longing" (Rom. 8:19) for the culmination of God's New Creation. This New Age, which Paul felt God had begun in Christ, was the hope and expectation of the inspired Jewish writers.

CONCLUSION

We have seen that the former assertion that Paul believed the Law to be dead left readers with the puzzling observation that Paul was also urging adherence to laws of God or of Christ. When one realizes that the Torah was a divine revelation for Paul, and that it endured, it becomes evident that he has applied the Torah's moral and ethical precepts to life in the church. In other words, "living in the Spirit results in obeying the Law."[17] Because Gentiles did not have to become Jews in order to be in Christ, Paul made no effort to encourage compliance with the Torah's cultic or dietary requirements.

The lifestyle which Paul did promote, then, was one described by the Torah, but Paul urged Gentile conformity to that lifestyle because they would thereby imitate Christ. Raised within the Jewish tradition which looked for the completion of God's creation and which saw Adam as a symbol of a unified humanity, Paul applied these concepts to Christ.

Christ was the beginning of the New Creation. His death for others was the ultimate sign that he was in God's image and was, therefore, a new Adam/Man. His for-others, Godlike lifestyle was understood to become the lifestyle of his followers who live in his Spirit. Such followers of Christ, living a human life in God's image, form a saved community. Patterned after Jewish notions of the saved covenantal community, the community living in Jesus' Spirit contrasts dramatically with the warped and distorted humanity of the outside world. Those in Christ (like those in the Torah-covenant) were saved and so lived according to God's designs.

And so it becomes apparent how much of Paul's thought is a logical extension of Jewish theology. His treatment of "law" is reasonable and quite powerful when appreciated within its Jewish context. Unfortunately, "after his day, when his letters came to read by Gentiles who little understood Judaism, the misinterpretation of Paul became almost inevitable."[18]

It has also been noted that Paul, as Apostle to the Gentiles, addressed non-Jews with his gospel of God's mercy through Christ. Paul's thoughts about his fellow-Jews who did not come to believe in Christ must now be considered.

Questions for Reflection and Discussion

1. Does the idea that the Old Testament understands God to be a God of love come as a surprise to you? Why or why not?

2. Noting the similarities between the Law of Moses (Torah) and the Law of Christ, what are their differences?

3. How might the rabbinic idea of Adam as a symbol of a reunited humanity be useful or be realized in the future?

4. For Paul, Christ was the perfect human, someone living in God's image. How might this concept relate to this expression: "Christ was super-human"?

5. For Christians, is *belief* in Christ all that is needed to be saved or are there any "commandments" that should be fulfilled?

CHAPTER FIVE

The Law's End or Its Confirmation?

THE NEW MESSIANIC AGE

In the preceding chapter Paul's conception of Christ as the beginning of the long-awaited New Creation was discussed. This New Creation, also called the New Age, the Age to Come, or the Messianic Age, would see the realization of God's full intentions for his creation. Part of that ultimate fulfillment of God's designs was understood to include the restoration of a unified humanity as symbolized in the person of Adam. Paul is convinced, as previously noted, that through Christ all people can now be accounted righteous. Both Jew and Greek can receive adoption as God's children; humanity can finally be united under the loving parent-like care of its Creator.

Although we have already seen that Paul believed the Messianic Age had begun in Christ, it has not yet been pointed out that he thinks the New Age would be fully realized with

Christ's triumphant return. The return of Christ, his *parousia* (par-oo-see'-ah), would herald the final in-breaking of God's Reign:

> For as in Adam all die, so also in Christ shall all be made alive. But each in his own order: Christ the first fruits, then at his coming those who belong to Christ. Then comes the end, when he delivers the kingdom to God the Father after destroying every rule and every authority and every power. . . .When all things are subjected to him, then the Son himself will also be subjected to him who put all things under him, that God may be everything to everyone" (1 Cor. 15:23-24;28).

With the *parousia* of Christ, civil governments and authorities would be unnecessary since all the world would be living under the kingship of the one God of all.

Most significantly, Paul expects Jesus to return very soon![1] In 1 Thess. 4:13-18, Paul writes to console church members who grieve because their loved ones have died before Christ has returned. Paul assures them that the dead in Christ will be raised on the day of the *parousia*. The concern of the Thessalonians shows that they seem surprised at the delay of Christ's coming, a sign that Paul had preached his imminent return.[2] Indeed, 1 Thess. 4:15, "We who are still alive ..." indicates that Paul feels the *parousia* will occur in his own lifetime.

He is not so sure of that in Phil. 1:21-26 where he wonders if it is preferable to remain alive or to die "and be with Christ." Still, he thinks his readers will be alive at Christ's coming since he exhorts them to keep "holding to the word of life so that in the day of Christ I may be proud that I did not run in vain or labor in vain" (2:16).

Remarks in other letters also point to Paul's belief in the imminence of Christ's *parousia*. In 1 Cor. 7 Paul states that "in view of the impending distress" (vs. 26), because "the appointed time has grown very short" (29), and since "the form of this world is passing away" (31), no one should live their everyday lives as they did previously (vss. 26-30). This sense of shortness of time is also found in Paul's last letter. In Rom.

13:11-12 he writes, "You know what hour it is, how it is full time now to wake from sleep. For salvation is nearer to us now than when we first believed; the night is far gone, the day is at hand."

This idea that the Messianic Age was rushing to its fulfillment at great speed has implications for Paul's discussion of Jews not in Christ, as will be seen. It should also be noted, however, that if, for Paul, Christ is the New Man, then the church is the new and reunited humanity of the Age to Come.

THE CHURCH: THE MESSIANIC COMMUNITY

This conception of church as the people of the Messianic Age can be clearly seen in Galatians 3:27-28:

> For as many of you as were baptized into Christ have put on Christ. There is neither Jew nor Greek, there is neither slave nor free, there is neither male nor female; for you are all one in Christ Jesus.

There is widespread scholarly agreement that these verses are an early baptismal formula which Paul has quoted. It seems likely that newcomers into the church heard these or similar words prayed or chanted during the ritual of baptism. [3]

The formula shows that the early church saw itself as beyond the divisive distinctions which tear humanity apart. As we have seen, Paul's central concern was to ensure the place of Gentiles in the community, and there is evidence he also believed in equal membership rights for slaves and women. *

It is important to realize that membership in Christ did not eliminate one's Jewishness/Gentileness or free/slave status

---

* The letter to Philemon illustrates Paul's concern with a slave named Onesimus whom Paul accepts as a brother in Christ. The baptismal formula should also give pause to those who depict Paul as "the eternal enemy of women." [4] Just as Paul's Jewishness has been neglected so, too, his attitude toward women has been misunderstood. Readers should note that almost all of the sexist language attributed to Paul is found in letters now realized to have been written decades after his death. [5] Furthermore, Paul calls many women (such as Phoebe, Junia, Priscilla, Euodia, and Syntyche) by such titles and descriptions as ministers, apostles, teachers, fellow-workers, and prophets. [6] Paul's equal regard for both women and men in the church indicates he really believes that in Christ all are one.

or their masculinity/femininity, rather such distinctions were to be irrelevant in the church where all were equally one.[7] Thus, Jews in Christ still continued to observe the Torah and thereby remained Jews, while Gentiles did not cease being Gentiles by becoming Jewish. Slaves remained slaves in the outside world, but in Christ were equal to everyone else (1 Cor. 7:21-23). Women remained women and men remained men, should comport themselves as such (1 Cor. 11:1-16), but were equals in Christ: "For as woman was made from man, so man is now born from woman. And all things are from God" (11:12).[8]

With these thoughts in mind, namely, that Christ was expected to return soon and that the church was the new humanity in which differences existed but were irrelevant, we now turn to Paul's thoughts about his Jewish brethren and his hopes for the future.

THE LETTER TO THE ROMANS

Our discussion of Paul in the preceding three chapters indicated that his main concern was with the Gentiles. Practically all of his letters were written to Gentiles about Gentile problems, bringing a message of new-found salvation specifically for Gentiles.

The letter to the Romans is in many ways unique among the Pauline epistles. It is the only message Paul sent to a church community he did not personally found. In addition, unlike many of his other letters, Paul seems to have taken his time in writing this one. Here he offers a more balanced and well-thought-out presentation of his gospel than is found in the fiery and angry letter to the Galatians, for example. More importantly for our purposes, Romans is the only letter in which Paul clearly addresses Jews in Christ and in which he discusses those Jews who have not come to acknowledge Jesus as Lord.

There are several reasons why Jews receive Paul's attention in his letter to the Roman church. This community seems to have been founded by Jewish believers in Jesus from Jerusalem, possibly as soon as the mid-40s.[9] The church which developed in Rome was probably mostly Jewish in its original composition. (There were about 50,000 Jews in Rome at the time).[10] Such a church would therefore represent a quite Jewish form of belief in Jesus, not unlike that of the mother church in Jerusalem.[11] The Roman church would be far more rooted in Judaic traditions than the predominantly Gentile Pauline communities, even though Gentiles subsequently joined the Roman church in significant numbers (note that in Rom. 1: 13-15, Paul compares those in Rome with "the rest of the Gentiles"). When Paul writes to this community, then, he must address both Jews and Gentiles, a situation he has not really faced before.

Paul has written to the believers in Rome not only because he hopes to visit them en route to Spain (15:24,28), but also to enlist their support on his behalf when he returns to the Jerusalem church with financial aid from the Gentile communities (15:25-27, 30-31). It is possible that those in Jerusalem have heard rumors that Paul is encouraging Jews to cease Torah-observance,* so Paul is hoping that the Roman community, with its Jerusalem-like esteem for Judaism, will put in a good word for him with the mother-church before he returns there.[12]

And so it is because of the background of his Roman addressees that Paul for the first time discusses Jews both in and outside of Christ. His comments on the subject are absolutely crucial for our exploration of the Jewishness of Paul.

PAUL'S CRITICISM OF HIS FELLOW JEWS

Paul begins his Roman correspondence by devoting several chapters to proving that all humanity is "under the power of sin" (3:9). He first discusses the situation of the Gentiles who, before they were in Christ, "did not see fit to acknowledge God" (1:28), and so were "without excuse" (1:20) for all their sinful deeds (1:22-32). He ends this section with one of those confusing sentences in which "law" has multiple meanings. Based on our previous examination of the term, 2:12 should probably be understood to mean, "All who have sinned in lawlessness will also perish since they do not have the Law,

---

* The letter to the Galatians can give that impression. Recall, too, that Paul is charged with this in Acts 21:20-21.

and all who have sinned while under the Law's curse will be judged (and presumably condemned) by the Law." Both the lawless and those "under the Law" in this verse are Gentiles. Comments addressed to Jews do not start until verse 17.

"But if you call yourself a Jew and rely upon the Law ..." (2:17) begins several paragraphs written to Paul's Jewish brethren. After remarking about boasts, knowledge, and instruction in vss. 17-18 (topics harshly addressed in 1 Cor.), Paul asks if Jews can really be certain if they are following the Law (vss. 21-24). He obviously thinks that they have in some way failed to live up to the Torah, but he doesn't yet specify the offense.

After noting that "circumcision is indeed of value if you obey the Law" (2:25) and that Jews have great advantages over Gentiles (3:1-2), he goes on to assert that despite this Jews, too, are sinful and must rely on God's mercy (3:9-20).

But now the main point is made. Some Jews are unfaithful (3:3) because they have failed to see that "now the righteousness of God has been manifest *apart* from the Law, although the Law and the prophets bear witness to it—the righteousness of God through faith in Jesus Christ for all who believe" (3:21).

Speaking as a Jew, Paul continues:

> Then what becomes of our boasting? It is excluded.
> On what principle? On the principle of works? No,
> but on the principle of faith. For we hold that a man
> is justified by faith apart from works of law. Or is
> God the God of the Jews only? Is he not the God of
> the Gentiles also? Yes, of Gentiles also, since God
> is one; and he will justify the circumcised on the
> ground of their faith and the uncircumcised through
> their faith. Do we then overthrow the Law by this
> faith? By no means! On the contrary, we uphold the
> Law (3:27-31).

This passage is extremely significant. "We hold that a man is justified by faith" without doing "the Law" (vs. 28) means that it has become possible through Christ for Gentiles to be adopted as God's own people *without* entering into the Torah-covenant because God is God of Jews and Gentiles alike (vs. 29). Jews have always been accounted righteous because of their faith-response to the God of Abraham, and now Gentiles may become righteous through their faith in Christ (vs. 30). However, Paul feels that those Jews who deny what God has now done in Christ have ceased having faith that the promises in the Torah would be realized.[13]

Paul argues this point by insisting that this new development is consistent with the Torah (vs. 31). He reminds his Jewish brothers and sisters that faith has always been the prerequisite for salvation and that the Law is simply an expression of that faith (4:1-15). God's promises to Abraham are "guaranteed to all his descendants—not only to adherents of the Law but also to those who share in the faith of Abraham" (4:16). The faith of Gentiles can and does exist for Paul, even though they do not manifest it by means of Torah-observance. Gentiles exhibit their faith by living the loving lifestyle of Christ, a lifestyle which embodies the Torah but which is distinct from it.*

Paul's criticism of his fellow Jews outside of Christ is very specific. It is not, as has been alleged for centuries, that the Jews have failed to realize the futility of their religion which has now been voided and supplanted by Christ. Such an attitude is utterly impossible for a man who upholds the Torah traditions as we have seen.

No, Paul's critique is expressed in Rom. 9:30-32a:

> What shall we say, then? That the Gentiles who did not pursue righteousness have attained it, that is righteousness through faith; but that Israel pursuing the Law of righteousness did not reach it. Why? Because [they saw the sign of righteousness] not as faith but as of works."**

Paul believes that his fellow Jews cannot imagine that one could

---

* Paul discusses this point at length in Romans 5 through 8.

** This rendition of verse 32 has been translated very literally from the Greek to show how all translations must insert extra terms in order for the sentence to make sense [done here in brackets]. If the translator is influenced by a belief that the Law is dead, the words he or she adds are affected accordingly. Those supplied here are based on the train of thought in 3:27-31, namely, that faith can be real (and effective for accepting God's offer of righteousness) even if not manifested by Torah-observance.

be righteous in God's sight without manifesting that righteousness by living according to the Torah. Thus they cannot see the faith in the God of Abraham through Christ which the Gentiles possess because the Gentiles are apart from works of the Law.

It was in this sense that Paul argues that the Law became a veil to hide Christ (2 Cor. 3:14-15). By so zealously observing Torah, Paul's brethren became blinded to the possibility of another form of righteousness distinct from the Torah. Recall that Paul himself had suffered from the same myopia before his calling.

Paul also expresses this criticism in another way. His brethren have failed to see that "Christ is the goal of the Law, that everyone who has faith may be justified" (Rom. 10:4). This phrase has been consistently misunderstood because of negative Christian assumptions about the continuing legitimacy of Judaism. The Greek word *telos* is usually translated as *end*, and thus "Christ is the *end* of the Law." *End*, in English, can mean the termination of something, and so this passage has been generally understood to mean Christ had abolished the Law.* If Paul really believed this how could he say, "The Law is holy and the commandment is holy and good and just" (Rom. 7:12), or "We uphold the Law" (3:31)?

The Greek *telos* means end in the sense of purpose or goal or something-sought-after. Thus, Christ is the Law's goal; he is the confirmation of the Law's promises that all humanity would find blessing in Abraham (and in Abraham's God). "All of the promises of God find their Yes in him" (2 Cor. 1:20). Rather than being the termination of the Torah, Paul believes that Christ is the ultimate expression of Torah lifestyle—an expression which makes Israel a light to the nations and extends God's Way to all the world. Far from calling down the curtain on the Law's final act, so to speak, Christ is raising the curtain on a new act in the Torah's unfolding drama—an act in which the entire world becomes its stage.[14]

Paul is saddened because many of his fellow Jews have

---

* Such a notion is also contrary to evidence from the ministry of Jesus himself. For example, note Matt. 5:17, "Think not that I have come to abolish the Law and the prophets; I have not come to abolish them but to fulfill them."

failed to see this new thing God has done which Paul has come to understand. Paul sees them as avoiding fellowship with the Gentiles and seeking to perpetuate the barriers which divide humanity. (It should once again be observed that Paul does not wish to annihilate Jewishness so that all people are one as non-Jews. He asserts, rather, that in Christ Jews are Jews in fellowship with Gentiles.) But by being blind to God's dramatic new actions in Christ (the subject of Romans 9-10), Paul feels that some Jews are hindering God's plans to reunify humanity.

PAUL'S VIEW OF THE FUTURE

We come to the pivotal passages in the letter to the Romans. [15] In Chapter 11 Paul wrestles with his dismay over his fellow Jews' lack of vision and expresses his hopes and fears for the future.

He concludes that the opposition of his fellow Jews is part of God's plan. "Through their trespass salvation has come to the Gentiles, so as to make Israel jealous. . . .Inasmuch as I am an apostle to the Gentiles I magnify my ministry in order to make my fellow Jews jealous and thus save some of them" (vss. 11b, 13b,14). Paul suggests that God has intended Jewish resistance in order to give the Gentiles the opportunity to become part of the Messianic community. Convinced that eventually the Jews will see the Gentiles' faith as a true manifestation of God's will, Paul is sure they will also therefore rejoice in it. And "what will their acceptance mean but life from the dead" (vs. 15b)!

Paul's use of the phrase "and thus save some of them" sounds as if he thinks that unless Jews believe in Christ they are not saved. However, he makes clear in no uncertain terms that such is not his view: "I ask, then, has God rejected his people? By no means!"(11:1); "So I ask, have they stumbled so as to fall? By no means!" (11:11a); "As regards the gospel they are enemies of God for your sake; but as regards election they are beloved for the sake of their forefathers. For the gifts and the call of God are irrevocable" (11:28-29).

Paul leaves little room for doubt. He is completely

satisfied that despite their current intransigence, Jews were and
remained God's people because of the irrevocability of their
election. In the short time left before the End of the Age, their
obstinacy has sparked the spread of the gospel to the Gentiles.
Paul does what he can to save them from their error, but the
ultimate salvation of Israel is without question. God who is
faithful to his word has promised that "all Israel will be
saved" (11:26).

The discussion of the Election of Israel seems to result
from some anti-Jewish rhetoric which is beginning to be heard
among the Gentiles in Christ. "Lest you be wise in your own
conceits, I want you to understand this mystery..." (11:25a)
is how Paul begins his summary of the reasons for Israel's
faltering and the certitude of her ultimate salvation. It appears
that Paul is beginning to wonder if the church might, in fact,
become a purely Gentile community. He fears that if this
happens that traditional Gentile anti-Jewish sentiment might
result in an even wider rift between the church and Israel. He
issues this strong warning:

> Now I am speaking to you Gentiles. Inasmuch then
> as I am an apostle to the Gentiles, I magnify my
> ministry in order to make my fellow Jews jealous and
> thus save some of them. For if their rejection means
> the reconciliation of the world, what will their
> acceptance mean but life from the dead? If the dough
> offered as first fruits is holy, so is the whole lump;
> and if the root is holy so are the branches. But if some
> of the branches were broken off, and you, a wild
> olive shoot, were grafted in their place to share the
> richness of the olive tree, do not boast over the
> branches. If you do boast, remember that it is not
> you that supports the root, but the root that supports
> you. You will say, "Branches were broken off so that
> I might be grafted in." That is true. They were broken
> off because of their unbelief, but you stand fast only
> through faith. So do not become proud, but stand
> in awe. For if God did not spare the natural branches,
> neither will he spare you. Note then the kindliness
> and the severity of God: severity toward those who
> have fallen, but God's kindness to you provided you

continue in his kindness; otherwise you too will be cut off. And even the others, if they do not persist in their unbelief, will be grafted in again, for God has the power to graft them in again. For if you have been cut from what is by nature a wild olive tree, and grafted, contrary to nature, into a cultivated olive tree, how much more will these natural branches be grafted back into their own olive tree.

Lest you be wise in your own conceits, I want you to understand this mystery, brethren: a hardening has come upon part of Israel, until the full number of the Gentiles come in, and so all Israel will be saved . . . .As regards the gospel they are enemies of God, for your sake; but as regards election they are beloved for the sake of their forefathers. For the gifts and the call of God are irrevocable (11:13-26a,28-29).

There are some deep and profound meanings in this passage which may not be immediately obvious. Paul's choice of the olive tree for his metaphor is interesting. Typically, the vine or the vineyard is the usual image used to describe God's People. But Paul has used the olive tree apparently for this reason: only the cultivated olive tree produces fruit; no olive oil can be made from the wild olive.[16]

The Gentiles, artificially grafted onto the olive tree of Israel, will only live and produce fruit so long as they are in unity with their Jewish roots. Their life is possible only because of the faith of their Jewish predecessors. No boasting over those Jewish branches which have become separated from God's unfolding plan is conceivable. Not only is the Gentiles' life with God dependent on their Jewish roots, those Jewish branches which were cut off to make room for the Gentiles are irrevocably destined to be re-incorporated into a completely unified tree—a tree in which all branches, despite their different origins and ways of growth, are offshoots of Abraham and heirs of God's incomprehensible graciousness.

CONCLUSION

The letter to the Romans is a summary of Paul's theological reflections. As we had already noted, Paul believes that a New

Age has begun in Christ. Gentiles through faith in Christ may become adopted heirs of Abraham and children of God. They may enter into a Messianic or saved community as full equals with Jews who had already been justified by God's mercy in their election. Thus, Christ is clearly the goal of the Torah, the confirmation of all the Torah's promises regarding the salvation of the Gentiles.

Paul's criticism of his fellow Jews who do not have faith in Christ is quite specific. Although they are good, holy, and zealous people destined for salvation, they are not being faithful to that aspect of the Torah which promised the eventual inclusion of the Gentiles in the saved community. They cannot imagine that God could account the Gentiles righteous by a new and dramatic means distinct from, though in confirmation of, the Torah.

Upset and puzzled by this tunnel-vision, which had been his own earlier failing, Paul concludes that his brethren's error has resulted in a more rapid spread of the gospel to the Gentiles, thereby furthering God's plan. God must have intended Jewish resistance to catalyze the proliferation of the gospel message because the time was very short before Jesus' return. This idea makes greater sense when the modern reader recalls Paul's first-century world view (the then known world was quite small compared to its actual dimensions) and his belief that the Age to Come was imminent. In the short time left, the temporarily confounded Jews had permitted a hastened proclamation of salvation to the Gentile nations.

Paul also came to suspect that the church might possibly end up as a completely Gentile community. Perhaps having heard some anti-Jewish polemic from Gentiles in Christ, he sternly warned them to realize that their salvation depended on their grateful acceptance of incorporation into Israel. Conceit and boasting over the elder Chosen People could not be part of those living in Christ. Just as Gentiles had benefited from God's covenantal promises to Abraham, so God also irrevocably loves and saves Israel.

Paul's fears about an exclusively Gentile church's hostility to Judaism proved to be foresighted indeed. The Gentile church came to distort and twist his own words against the

People and the Torah he loved. This modern awareness and the rediscovery of the gospel of the Jewish Apostle to the Gentiles has tremendous ramifications which the next chapter will explore.

Questions for Reflection and Discussion

1. Paul envisioned Christ as the New Adam and the church to be the beginning of a unified humanity. Now, two thousand years later, to what extent are these ideas realized or unrealized?

2. How is Christ the confirmation of the Law in terms of God's promises to Israel?

3. Discuss Paul's conception that Jews in Christ continue to be Torah-observant people but now are in fellowship with Gentiles in Christ.

4. Why might Paul view the church's becoming an all-Gentile community as a potentially dangerous development?

5. What might Paul have to say about the structures and policies of the many Christian churches today?

CHAPTER SIX

Paul's Gospel Today

As previously mentioned, Paul's foreboding about an exclusively Gentile church was borne out by subsequent events. The Temple's destruction in the year 70 (a few years after Paul's death) greatly accelerated the separation of the church and the people Israel.

Some indication of this distancing can be seen in the gospel accounts of the crucifixion of Jesus. Although tortured and executed by Roman soldiers, there is a tendency in the gospels to excuse the Romans and blame Jesus' fellow Jews. The later the writing of the gospel, the more pronounced the tendency becomes.[1] Similarly, the Pharisees are depicted as far worse antagonists of Jesus than they likely were during his ministry in the early 30s. Of all the various groups existing at the time, Jesus may have had more in common with the Pharisaic renewal than with any other. Yet the Pharisees are portrayed much more negatively in gospels because, as the only major group to survive the Jewish-Roman War, it was they with whom the church was in conflict at the time the gospels were written.[2]

By the end of the first century, Gentile Christianity commonly expressed the view that Judaism had been replaced by the church. Christians were the adopted children of God and Jews were no longer God's Chosen People. As we have seen Paul, who trusted in God's faithfulness to his promise of covenant forever, would never condone such thinking. Nevertheless, Paul's own words were used to perpetuate the notion of the replacement of Judaism by Christianity. Since Christ was the "end" of the Law, it was natural for Christians to think that the destruction of the Temple was the sign of God's rejection of Israel (see Mt. 22:7, "...he sent his troops and destroyed those murderers and burned their city").

When in the fourth century Christianity came to control the civil government, Christians acquired the power to control Judaism by means of civil law. As time passed, Jews were legally restricted in terms of residence, occupation, and, from time to time, religious expression. It would ultimately be wondered why, if Judaism was rejected by God, the Jewish people had any right to exist at all.

As the centuries passed, Christianity increasingly reveled in its own divinely-favored status by developing negative stereotypes of Jews and Judaism. In this context Paul was universally understood as the great foe of the Judaism he had previously supported. His "conversion" showed him the futility of the Jewish Law because he finally understood that salvation could not be earned. He had traveled everywhere, it was believed, preaching the end of the hated Law to Gentile and Jew alike.

From the Jewish viewpoint, Christianity had become an oppressor. Faced with threats of submission to baptism or death, many Jews chose death out of faithfulness to Torah-covenant. Christian preaching that Judaism had become a fossil-like religion, meanwhile, was belied by the periodic flowering of Jewish spirituality under the inspiration of great rabbis. Yet the resultant increased Jewish commitment to the

Way of God in the Torah was seen by many Christians as further proof of the Jewish legalism and works-righteousness supposedly condemned by Paul. Despite courageous attempts by people of good will to bridge the Christian-Jewish chasm, the past 19 centuries have largely been characterized by the Christian oppression of Jews.

Paul's warning in Romans that Gentile disregard for the church's rootedness in Judaism would result in a severing of such Gentiles from God's Way came to a most horrifying reality in this century. As a result of a continuous history of anti-Jewish sentiment,* Christianity became in many ways a breeding ground for genocidal pogroms in various countries. The extermination of nine million people at the hands of people in nations which defined themselves as "Christian" must provoke all followers of Jesus to re-examine themselves. What could be further from the loving humanity in God's image described by the Torah and lived by Christ than the systematic elimination of a people among whom both Jesus and Paul would number themselves? Christians must ask themselves how their faith could have become so perverted to allow such evil. Must not they recognize that their Lord, the crucified Jew, would more likely identify himself with the Jewish victims than with their nominally "Christian" oppressors?

Furthermore, Paul's hope that the faith of Gentiles would cause his brethren to realize that God was at work among them has seldom had a chance to be tested. Rather than seeing God's Way reflected in the life of the Gentile church, Jews have most often seen oppression, hatred, and persecution instead.

Thankfully, there are signs today that a New Age may be dawning in which Christian-Jewish reconciliation might be possible. The Roman Catholic tradition, as part of its Second Vatican Council, issued a document which reversed 19 centuries of Christian preaching about Judaism. In the *Declaration on the Relationship of the Church to Non-Christian Religions*, the Roman church stated that Judaism had not been replaced by Christianity and that the Torah-covenant endures:

---

* As an illustration of this pervasive anti-Jewish sentiment, it might be noted that until the middle of this century Roman Catholics, in their Good Friday liturgy, prayed for "the perfidious Jews."

The Church, therefore, cannot forget that she received the revelation of the Old Testament through the people with whom God in his inexpressible mercy deigned to establish the Ancient Covenant. Nor can she forget that she draws sustenance from the root of that good olive tree onto which have been grafted the wild olive branches of the Gentiles (cf. Rom. 11:17-24). Indeed, the Church believes that by His cross Christ, our Peace, reconciled Jew and Gentile, making them both one in Himself (cf. Eph. 2:14-16).

Also, the Church ever keeps in mind the words of the Apostle about his kinsmen, "who have the adoption as sons, and the glory and the covenant and the legislation and the worship and the promises; who have the fathers, and from whom Christ is according to the flesh" (Rom. 9:4-5), the son of the Virgin Mary. The Church recalls too that from the Jewish people sprang the apostles, her foundation stones and pillars, as well as most of the early disciples who proclaimed Christ to the world.

As holy Scripture testifies, Jerusalem did not recognize the time of her visitation (cf. Lk. 19-44), nor did the Jews in large number accept the gospel; indeed, not a few opposed the spreading of it (cf. Rom. 11:28). Nevertheless, according to the Apostle, the Jews still remain most dear to God because of their fathers, for He does not repent of the gifts He makes nor of the calls He issues (cf. Rom. 11:28-29). In company with the prophets and the same Apostle, the Church awaits that day, known to God alone, on which all peoples will address the Lord in a single voice and "serve him with one accord" (Soph. 3:9; cf. Is. 66:23; Ps. 65:4; Rom. 11:11-32).*³

This reversed attitude has continued and grown up to the present. Such is evident in a speech given by Pope John Paul II to the Jewish community of West Germany on November 17, 1980. On that occasion the pope, referring to

---

* It is notable how often this document cites Paul, referred to as "the Apostle." Clearly a renewed understanding of his thought contributed to the discussions of the Council Fathers.

the Jewish people, called them "the people of the Old Covenant which has never been revoked."[4]

The ramifications of this highest offical preaching of the Roman church have yet to be fully appreciated, and there still exists a certain tension between this new perspective and the previous understanding. If the covenant of Abraham is still binding, then that must mean that Jews are still obligated to live by the Torah (as variously interpreted by different Jewish traditions), and that by so living for the last 19 centuries of Christian domination they have been faithful to God's will for them.[5] This presents a vexing dilemma to Christians who have come to feel that only they were God's people. How the Gentile church should relate to another, and elder, elect people is a major question facing Christianity today. Keeping the letter to the Romans in mind, it is a challenge to rediscover and to revere our Jewish forebears and their modern descendants, whose very existence is a testimony to God's faithfulness.

Jews also face a challenge in this new posture of the Roman church. If the Gentile churches do eventually redefine their self-understanding in terms of rootedness and support of Judaism's witness to God and his faithfulness (rather than in opposition to or as the replacement of Israel), will the people Israel come to accept that God has been at work in Christ? Such an acceptance would also involve some redefinition on Israel's part, but just as there are signs of hope in contemporary Christianity, there are also hopeful indications in modern Judaism.[6]

In any case, it appears that a New Age might indeed be possible for the dismembered peoples of God. All Christians, and especially preachers and catechists, must become aware of the continued holiness of their Jewish roots, and consciously avoid all language which perpetuates the earlier attitudes of replacement. Christians must confess, repent, and forever disavow their hateful history and experience the true conversion of heart that their Lord requires. Jews must be willing to accept such repentance as sincere, have courage enough to trust again despite centuries of contrary evidence, and be open to listening to the church's rediscovered appreciation of its Jewishness. They must also be ready to consider the possibility that God's will has been done in the formation of the Gentile church and that Christians are indeed younger Chosen People.

Perhaps Paul, although he must be understood in his first century context, can provide some direction in the modern quest for Jewish-Christian reconciliation. Living in a time when Jews and Gentiles were both in Christ, yet remaining Jew and Gentile, and himself being an observant Jew, Paul's profound understanding of the gospel requires serious attention today. Christian theological and christological language formed during the late first century church-synagogue disputes should perhaps be de-emphasized and Pauline concepts stressed instead. The Jewish apostle to the Gentiles clearly possessed valuable insights on the significance of Christ, a perspective that could be extremely fruitful today:

> I tell you that Christ became a servant to the Jewish people in the cause of God's truthfulness, in order to confirm the promises made to the patriarchs and in order that the Gentiles might glorify God for his mercy (Rom. 15:8-9).

Questions for Reflection and Discussion

1. Which do you think would be easier to accomplish: (a) redirecting Christian thinking to acknowledge its Jewishness, or (b) the people Israel coming to accept that God has been at work in Christ?

2. What are some ways in which Jewish-Christian reconciliation can be fostered? What might hinder this?

3. To what extent has cultural anti-Judaism, both presently and in past generations, influenced the interpretation and the understanding of the Sacred Scriptures?

4. From a Jewish perspective, discuss Christianity as the oppressor.

5. In the late first century the early church writers emphasized the growing hostility between Judaism and Christianity. What should be the emphasis of the late 20th century to creatively respond to the new insights about the teachings of Paul?

Notes

1. For more information of the origins of the modern biblical movement see Raymond E. Brown, "Our New Approach to the Bible," in *New Testament Essays* (New York: Image Books, 1968), pp. 21-35.

2. For an easily-understood introduction to the parables of Jesus see John W. Miller, *Step By Step Through the Parables* (New York: Paulist Press, 1981).

3. Vatican Council II, *Dogmatic Constitution on Divine Revelation*, 12, translated by Walter M. Abbott (New York: Guild Press, 1966.)

4. For more information on the various research techniques used by contemporary Scripture scholars see Raymond F. Collins, *Introduction to the New Testament* (Garden City, N.Y.: Doubleday, 1983).

5. For very easy reading of the overall modern scriptural viewpoint see two books: Melvin L. Farrell, *Getting to Know the Bible* (Milwaukee: Hi-Time Publ., 1984); and James F. Leary, *A Light to the Nations* (New Jersey: Arena Lettres, 1983).

6. Geza Vermes, *Jesus the Jew* (Philadelphia: Fortress Press, 1981), pp. 46-48.

7. Gerd Theissen, *Sociology of Early Palestinian Christianity* (Philadelphia: Fortress Press, 1977), pp. 49-51, 63.

8. Theissen, *Sociology*, p. 48.

9. Ben Meyer, *The Aims of Jesus* (London, SCM Press, 1979), p. 173.

10. Theissen, *Sociology*, pp. 103-110.

11. Meyer, *Aims of Jesus*, pp. 129-179.
    For two modern and very readable explorations of Jesus' ministry, see Gerald S. Sloyan, *Jesus in Focus: A Life in Its Setting* (Mystic, Conn.: Twenty-Third Publications, 1983), and Donald Senior, *Jesus: A Gospel Portrait* (Dayton, Ohio: Pflaum Press, 1975).

12. Robert Jewett, *A Chronology of Paul's Life* (Philadelphia: Fortress Press, 1979), pp. 26-29.

13. Raymond E. Brown, *The Virginal Conception and Bodily Resurrection of Jesus* (New York: Paulist Press, 1973), pp. 108-110.

14. For a nice introduction to Judaism today see Edward Zerin, *What Catholics (And Other Christians) Should Know About Jews* (Dubuque, Iowa: W.C. Brown Group, 1980).

15. Walter Schmithals, *Paul and James* (London: SCM Press, 1965), p. 19; Gunther Bornkamm, *Paul* (New York: Harper and Row, 1971), p. 14.

16. Besides the reference in Acts 8:4 ff., there is evidence of an early successful mission to Samaria in the Gospel of John. See Raymond E. Brown, *The Community of the Beloved Disciple* (New York: Paulist Press, 1979), pp. 36-40.

17. Raymond E. Brown and John Meier, *Antioch and Rome* (New York: Paulist Press, 1983), pp. 97-104.

18. For an excellent overview of Jewish history see Abba Eban, *Heritage: Civilization and the Jews* (New York: Summit Books, 1984).

19. Bornkamm, *Paul*, pp. 8-10.

20. Eban, *Heritage*, p. 98.

21. John C. Meagher, "As the Twig Was Bent: Anti-Semitism in Greco-Roman and Early Christian Times," in *Anti-Semitism and the Foundations of Early Christianity*, ed. Allen T. Davies (New York: Paulist Press, 1979), pp. 4-7.

22. For a rewarding, though lengthy, novelization of Jewish history which dramatically presents the Jewish struggle to preserve their covenant identity see James A. Michener, *The Source* (New York: Ballantine Books, 1965).

23. Eban, *Heritage*, pp. 79 and 84.

24. Bornkamm, *Paul*, pp. 6-8.

25. This quote is from the Jewish historian Josephus cited by Wayne A. Meeks and Robert L. Wilken, *Jews and Christians in Antioch in the First Four Centuries of the Common Era* (Missoula, Montana: Scholars Press, 1978), p. 3.

26. Theissen, *Sociology*, p. 90; Bornkamm, *Paul*, p. 10.

27. Meagher, "As the Twig Was Bent," pp. 7-8.

28. Theissen, *Sociology*, p. 58.

29. Elisabeth Schussler Fiorenza, *In Memory of Her* (New York: Crossroads, 1983), pp. 175-183, 210.

30. Meeks & Wilken, *Jews and Christians in Antioch*, pp. 13-17.

31. Jewett, *Chronology*, pp. 90-91, 98-100.

32. W.D. Davies, *Jewish and Pauline Studies* (Philadelphia: Fortress Press, 1984), pp. 97-99; Clemens Thoma, *A Christian Theology of Judaism* (New York: Paulist Press, 1980), pp. 141-143.

33. For a concise description of the gradual separation of the Jesus-movement/Christianity from Judaism see David P. Efroymson, "Judaism and the Early Church," in *New Catholic Encyclopedia*, XVII, pp. 310-312.

34. This chart based substantially on Jewett, *Chronology of Paul's Life.*

35. Leander Keck, *Paul and His Letters* (Philadelphia: Fortress Press, 1979), pp. 3-4.

36. For more information on these pseudonymous or deutero-Pauline letters see Edward Schillebeeckx *Paul the Apostle* (New York: Crossroad, 1983), pp. 23-24; Raymond E. Brown, *The Churches the Apostles Left Behind* (New York: Paulist, 1984), pp. 20-22; Calvin Roetzel, *The Letters of Paul: Conversations in Context* (Atlanta: John Knox, 1982), 2nd ed., pp. 93-116.

37. The rendering here of the Greek *kata dikaiosynen tein en nomo* as "righteousness in the law" differs from the RSV's "under the law." Paul uses that phrase "under the law" ("hypo nomon") elsewhere (such as Gal. 3:23), but, as will be seen, he means something very specific by it. It will become clear that he does not have that meaning in mind in this Philippians passage; hence the alteration in the RSV's translation.

38. For more information on Paul's chronic disorder and its meaning see Krister Stendahl, *Paul Among Jews and Gentiles* (Philadelphia: Fortress Press, 1979), pp. 40-44.

CHAPTER TWO: *Conversion or Call?*

1. Stendahl, *Paul Among Jews and Gentiles*, p. 8; Bornkamm, *Paul*, p. 17.

2. Stendahl, *Paul Among Jews and Gentiles*, p. 10.

3. Paul M. van Buren, *A Christian Theology of the People Israel* (New York: Seabury, 1983), p. 146.

4. Davies, *Jewish and Pauline Studies*, p. 118.

5. van Buren, *Theology of People Israel*, p. 234.

6. W.D. Davies, *Paul and Rabbinic Judaism* (Philadelphia: Fortress Press, 1980), 4th ed., pp. 70-74.

This logic would also question the conclusion of John G. Gager, *The Origins of Anti-Semitism* (New York: Oxford University Press, 1983), pp. 201, 233-234, that Paul became an "apostate" Jew who ceased being Torah-observant in order to be more successful in winning Gentiles. Would James and the other Jerusalem leaders so readily extend the "right hand of fellowship" to one who had thus abandoned his Jewish identity, even if he never encouraged other Jews to do the same? Furthermore, would Gentile God-fearers, who admire Judaism, pay much heed to a self-proclaimed Law-breaker?

Gager's argument rests heavily on Gal. 2:17-18 and Phil. 3:8 where Paul speaks of "having died to the Law" and of his "former life in Judaism." Gager sees these passages as showing that Paul really did "convert" from Judaism (cf. pp. 209-210) by ceasing Torah-observance after encountering the Raised Lord. There is not only evidence to the contrary, as we have attempted to show, but Paul's remarks in Gal. 2:18-19 need not be understood as indicating Paul's complete disregard for Torah. Fellow Jews may have accused him of "dying to the Law" because of his close association with Gentile sinners. Paul, however, as will be seen in chapter 5, sees his actions as actually confirming the Law. His Galatian Judaizing opponents are no doubt using his apparent apostasy against him and Paul responds once again that it is not the Law that saves but acceptance of God's grace or gift of righteousness. Paul risks being ostracized by his brethren in order to fulfill his apostolic mission, but that need not be seen as a cessation of Torah-life.

7. Bornkamm, *Paul*, pp. 15-16.

8. Davies, *Jewish and Pauline Studies*, pp. 232-233.

9. Lloyd Gaston, "Paul and the Torah," in *Anti-Semitism and the Foundations of Early Christianity*, p. 52; Stendahl, *Paul Among Jews and Gentiles*, p. 2.

10. van Buren, *Theology of People Israel*, pp. 232-233; Stendahl, *Paul Among Jews and Gentiles*, p. 9.

11. That some Jews were becoming increasingly sensitive to a loss of self-identity is argued by James D.G. Dunn, "The Incident at Antioch (Gal. 2: 11-18)," in *Journal for the Study of the New Testament*, 18, (1983), pp. 10-11.

12. The preceding sentences are not meant to suggest that Paul, before his calling, hated or despised Gentiles. If Acts 22:3 is historically valid and Paul became a Pharisee under the tutelage of Rabbi Gamaliel the Elder, then he would have learned the Torah according to the traditions of the school of Hillel, Gamaliel's grandfather. Hillel taught that a Gentile who observed the Noahide commandments (the basis of Acts 15:20)

would be righteous in the world to come (see Harvey Falk *Jesus the Pharisee*, [New York: Paulist, 1985,] p. 26.) Thus, Paul would be expected to believe that righteousness was possible (though perhaps unlikely, see Rom. 1:18-2:16) among the Gentiles. But sharing table-fellowship with such Gentiles might seem a little too easy-going to Paul, especially if he had knowledge of Stephen's statements in Jerusalem and took them to be representative of the Jesus-movement. Peter's actions in Antioch, then, would have reminded Paul of his own past views, partially accounting for his vehemence.

13. Bornkamm, *Paul*, p. 16.

14. Stendahl, *Paul Among Jews and Gentiles*, p. 89.

Chapter Three: *Salvation for the Gentiles*

---

1. Gaston, "Paul and the Torah," pp. 49-51; E.P. Sanders, *Paul and Palestinian Judaism* (Philadelphia: Fortress Press, 1979), pp. 1-59.

2. Throughout van Buren, *Theology of People Israel*, there are such implications. See also Thoma, *Christian Theology of Judaism*, pp. 173-176.

3. Sanders, *Paul and Palestinian Judaism*, p. 85.

4. van Buren, *Theology of People Israel*, p. 76.

5. Sanders, *Paul and Palestinian Judaism*, p. 426.

6. Sanders, *Paul and Palestinian Judaism*, pp. 147, 157.

7. Davies, *Jewish and Pauline Studies*, p. 18.

8. Sanders, *Paul and Palestinian Judaism*, p. 205.

9. van Buren, *Theology of People Israel*, pp. 72-77.

10. Davies, *Jewish and Pauline Studies*, p. 18.

11. Thoma, *Christian Theology of Judaism*, p. 98.

12. Sanders, *Paul and Palestinian Judaism*, p. 422.

13. Lloyd Gaston, "Israel's Enemies in Pauline Theology," *New Testament Studies*, 28 (1982), p. 401.

14. van Buren, *Theology of People Israel*, p. 106.

15. Gaston, "Paul and the Torah," p. 56.

16. Gaston, "Paul and the Torah," pp. 62-65.

17. See Vincent P. Branick, "The Sinful Flesh of the Son of God (Rom. 8:3): A Key Image in Pauline Theology," *The Catholic Biblical Quarterly*, 47 (1985), pp. 246-262.

18. Gaston, "Paul and the Torah," p. 62.

19. van Buren, *Theology of People Israel*, p. 126.

20. Gaston, "Paul and the Torah," p. 63.

21. van Buren, *Theology of People Israel*, p. 126.

22. Gaston, "Paul and the Torah," pp. 60-61.

23. van Buren, *Theology of People Israel*, pp. 126-127.

24. Lloyd Gaston, "Angels and Gentiles in Early Judaism and in Paul," *Sciences Religieuses/Studies in Religion*, 11/1 (1982), pp. 65-75.

25. van Buren, *Theology of People Israel*, pp. 145-147, 232-234.

26. Gaston, "Israel's Enemies in Pauline Theology," pp. 405-410.

27. Stendahl, *Paul Among Jews and Gentiles*, p. 37.

CHAPTER FOUR: *Gentiles in Christ*

1. E.P. Sanders, *Paul, the Law and the Jewish People* (Philadelphia: Fortress Press, 1984), p. 106, raises this question. The issue is never fully resolved because of Sander's assertion that Paul believes the Torah has come to an end. (Cf. Gager, *Origins of Anti-Semitism*, pp. 203-204, 207.)

2. Stendahl, *Paul Among Jews and Gentiles*, p. 37.

3. Davies, *Paul and Rabbinic Judaism*, pp. 117-118, 129-131.

4. Jerome Murphy-O'Connor, *Becoming Human Together: The Pastoral Anthropology of St. Paul* (Wilmington, Delaware: Michael Glazier, 1982), pp. 184-186.

5. Davies, *Jewish and Pauline Studies*, pp. 281-283.

6. Murphy-O'Connor, *Becoming Human Together*, pp. 169-170.

7. Sanders, *Paul and Palestinian Judaism*, p. 427. See also pp. 147, 157.

8. Sanders, *Paul, the Law, and the Jewish People*, p. 111.

9. Murphy-O'Connor, *Becoming Human Together*, pp. 134-135.

10. Sanders, *Paul, the Law, and the Jewish People*, p. 102.

11. Murphy-O'Connor, *Becoming Human Together*, p. 33 ff. I am greatly indebted to Dr. O'Connor for many of the insights on the next four pages.

12. Davies, *Paul and Rabbinic Judaism*, p. 44.

13. van Buren, *Theology of People Israel*, pp. 55-56, 115.

14. Murphy-O'Connor, *Becoming Human Together*, pp. 207-211.

15. Davies, *Paul and Rabbinic Judaism*, pp. 51-57.

16. van Buren, *Theology of People Israel*, pp. 89-91.

17. Sanders, *Paul, the Law, and the Jewish People*, p. 105.

18. Davies, *Jewish and Pauline Studies*, p. 99.

CHAPTER FIVE: *The Law's End or Its Confirmation?*

---

1. Bornkamm, *Paul*, pp. 151, 221-222,238; Roetzel, *Conversations*, p. 51; Keck, *Letters*, p. 47.

2. Roetzel, *Conversations*, pp. 51-52.

3. Wayne A. Meeks, "The Image of the Androgyne: Some Uses of A Symbol in Earliest Christianity," *History of Religions*, 13 (1974), p. 182; Fiorenza, *In Memory of Her*, p. 208.

4. So said George Bernard as quoted in Elaine H. Pagels, "Paul and Women: A Response to a Recent Discussion," *Journal of the American Academy of Religion*, p. 42 (1972), p. 538.

5. Robin Scroggs, "Paul and the Eschatological Woman," *Journal of the American Academy of Religion*, 40 (1972), pp. 283-284.

6. See for example Romans 16:1-7,12; Phil. 4:2-3; 1 Cor. 11:5; Acts 18:1-3, 18-19,24-26.

7. Scroggs, "Eschatological Woman," pp. 288,293; Fiorenza, *In Memory of Her*, pp. 211,214; Meeks, "Androgyne," p. 202.

8. Jerome Murphy-O'Connor, "Sex and Logic in 1 Cor. 11:2-16," *Catholic Biblical Quarterly*, 42 (1980), pp. 482-501.

9. Brown and Meier, *Antioch and Rome*, pp. 101-103.

10. Eban, *Heritage*, p. 80.

11. Brown and Meier, *Antioch and Rome*, pp. 106,110.

12. Brown and Meier, *Antioch and Rome*, pp. 110-111,113.

13. Gager, *Origins of Anti-Semitism*, p. 217.

14. van Buren, *Theology of People Israel*, p. 233; C. Thomas Rhyne, "Nomos Dikaiosynes and the Meaning of Romans 10:4," *Catholic Biblical Quarterly*, 47 (1985), pp. 492-493, 499.; Gager, *Origins of Anti-Semitism*, p. 224.

15. Stendahl, *Paul Among Jews and Gentiles*, p. 4.

16. Davies, *Jewish and Pauline Studies*, pp. 154-157.

CHAPTER SIX: *Paul's Gospel Today*

---

1. Vatican Commission for Religious Relations with the Jews, "The Jews and Judaism in Preaching and Catechesis," *Origins*, Vol. 15 No. 7 (7/4/85), IV,21A, p. 106. For a sample of current scholarship on this topic see Hyam Z. Maccoby, "Jesus and Barabbas," *New Testament Studies*, 16 (1969-1970), pp. 55-60.

2. Vatican Commission, "Jews and Judaism," II 17,19, p. 105.

3. Vatican Council II, *Declaration on the Relationship of the Church to Non-Christian Religions*, 4. Translated by Walter M. Abbott (New York: Guild Press, 1966).

4. Vatican Commission, "Jews and Judaism," I,3, p. 103.

5. Note the statement by Eugene Fisher, Executive Director of the (U.S.) National Conference of Catholic Bishops' Secretariat for Jewish-Catholic

Relations, on June 24, 1985: "Jews since the time of Christ have continued to give faithful witness to the covenant and have continued to be a source of spiritual richness not only for Jews but for the world." *Origins*, Vol. 15 No. 7 (7/4/85), marginal note on p. 105.

6. Many Jewish scholars are writing insightfully about Christianity. Recently Rabbi Harvey Falk in his *Jesus the Pharisee* brought to light the opinion of Rabbi Jacob Emden (1697-1776) that Jesus intended to establish a new religion for the Gentiles based on the Noahide commandments (pp. 4-6, 13-23). While evidence from the gospels makes it clear that things are much more complex than that (see Mt. 15:24: "I was sent only to the lost sheep of the house of Israel," for instance), Falk's book is an example of how Jews are also striving to appreciate their cousins in Christ. van Buren's *A Christian Theology of the People Israel* is a stunning example of the reverse.

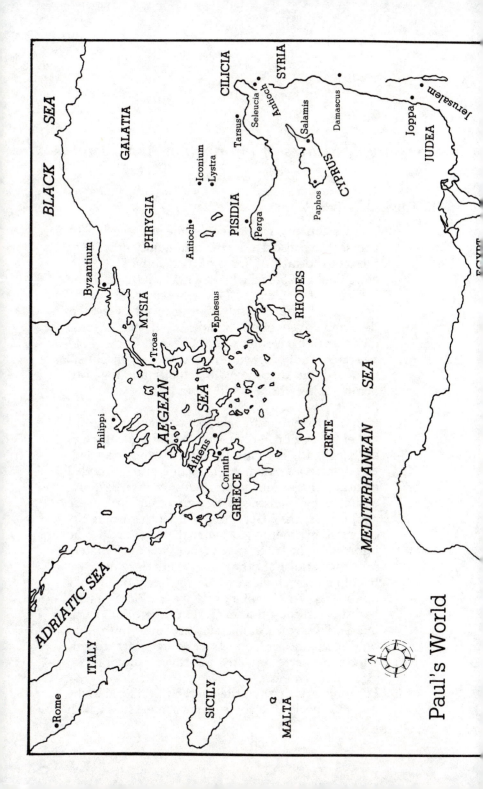

Paul's World

Summary of Sources of Information About Paul

I. The Letters Paul Wrote:

A. 1 Thessalonians, written sometime in the early 50s, was sent to console a church community upset over the recent deaths of some of its members. Apparently Paul had preached that Christ's return and the full commencement of God's Reign would occur very soon. The Thessalonians grieved over their departed loved ones, wondering if their deaths meant their exclusion from the Age to Come. Paul asserts that not only will "those who sleep in Christ" be raised, but that they will actually join the Lord before those who are still alive.

B. Galatians is not addressed to a particular city, but rather to a region in Asia Minor. Paul evidently was afflicted with his chronic illness while traveling through Galatia, and, while recuperating, founded a church there. This letter seems to have been occasioned by Paul receiving news that there were people pressuring Gentiles in Christ to become circumcised in order to guarantee their salvation. The impression the letter gives is that Paul immediately sat down and shot off an angry and fiery message to condemn such views. It is very likely that Paul's opponents were Gentile proselytes to Judaism who had superstitious and magical notions about earning God's favor. Paul argues that only faith, that only acceptance of God's grace as an unmerited gift, will incorporate one into the saved community.

C. Philippians written to the church in Philippi in the mid-50s, deals with some of the same issues which concerned Paul in Galatians. He warns his readers to be on guard against the "curs" encouraging circumcision. There is also internal dissension within the Philippian community, and Paul urges that followers of Jesus imitate their Lord who "emptied himself" and was totally in conformity with the will of God.

D. The Corinthian Letters, now known as 1st and 2nd Corinthians, are in reality fragments of three, four, or even five letters which have been edited into their present form. In Corinth there seems to have been an overly enthusiastic and extreme reaction to Paul's original preaching. Not only did the Corinthians accept that the Law was not binding on Gentiles, some apparently felt that they were now free to do whatever they wanted. There is evidence of immorality, gluttony, sexual deviations, and involvement with pagan temples and idols. There was fighting over who had the best spiritual gifts, who was the best apostle, and even over the eucharist. Furthermore, some Corinthians may have believed that they had already been raised to a glorified state of perfect freedom and wisdom. Paul insists that unless one lives in a life rooted in selfless love, everything else is a meaningless sham.

E. Philemon is the only authentic Pauline letter written to an individual. Philemon, a believer, owns a slave who has joined the church. Paul returns this slave to his master with a letter urging the slave's treatment as a beloved brother in Christ.

F. Romans, written in the late 50s, is Paul's only letter to a church he did not personally found and to a church with a mixed Jewish/Gentile membership. He seems to have written this letter to introduce himself to the long-established Roman church since he intended to visit there en route to Spain. He also might be seeking to give an accurate presentation of his preaching, since some foes were spreading distorted versions of what Paul had said. Most important, Paul in this letter makes clear that the Law is something "good and holy and just," and that he has not been encouraging Jews to become apostates. Rather, he emphasizes that through Christ God has now done something dramatic and new and "apart from the Law" in order to bring pagan Gentiles to himself. Paul criticizes his kinsfolk for failing to see this confirmation of Torah-promises, but he also warns Gentiles in Christ that they are only accounted righteous because of the Jewish root which makes them holy.

II. Acts of Apostles.

This companion volume to the Gospel of Luke was written by an admirer of Paul sometime in the 80s. It seeks to describe emerging Christianity as a natural outgrowth of Judaism which inevitably spread from Jerusalem to Rome. Paul figures predominantly in the second half of the book, but it seems that the author was more familiar with Paul's travel itinerary than with the content of Paul's preaching. Where Paul's letters and Acts disagree, greater weight is placed upon the letters.

III. Letters Written in Paul's Name

Many scholars consider that Ephesians, Colossians, 2 Thessalonians, and most certainly the Pastoral Epistles (1, 2 Timothy and Titus) were written decades after Paul's death by authors who considered themselves heirs to the Pauline tradition. They all show evidence of other concerns and differing theological perspectives which arose later in the first century. They preserve Pauline views with mixed success. Nevertheless, they are indirect sources of information about Paul.

A Comparison of Two Different Perspectives on Paul

PAUL AS "CHRISTIAN"	PAUL AS JEWISH APOSTLE TO GENTILES
converted away from Judaism to Christianity	called by God as apostle to the Gentile nations
ceased to follow the stifling Jewish Law	remained Torah-observant Jew throughout his life
realized that the Law was futile because no one could earn salvation	believed Jesus followed Torah as expression of thanks to the God who had chosen them as his people
rejoiced in being freed and liberated from enslavement under the Law	taught that Gentiles could now be freed from being under the Law's condemnation
taught that only through faith in Christ could one be made righteous	taught that through faith in Christ Gentiles could become adopted children of God and brothers/sisters of the Jews

Bibliography

(To make references more convenient all sources are combined alphabetically in this list, whether they are popularizations, scholarly works, or journal articles. Those titles recommended for popular reading, or which avoid over-technical language, are preceded by an asterisk and are followed by a short description of the work in parentheses.)

Bornkamm, Gunther. Paul. New York: Harper and Row, 1971.

Branick, Vincent P. "The Sinful Flesh of the Son of God (Rom. 8:3): A Key Image in Pauline Theology." Catholic Biblical Quarterly, 47 (1985), pp. 246-262.

* Brown, Raymond E. The Churches the Apostles Left Behind. New York: Paulist Press: 1984.
(This book considers seven church communities in the last third of the first century and examines how each of them coped differently with the deaths of eyewitnesses to Jesus' ministry.)

* _____. The Community of the Beloved Disciple. New York: Paulist Press, 1979.
(A reconstruction of the history of that church community in which were produced the gospel and letters of John.)

* _____. "Our New Approach to the Bible," in New Testament Essays. New York: Image Books, 1968, pp. 21-35.
(An essay which explains the causes of the modern scriptural movement.)

* _____. The Virginal Conception and the Bodily Resurrection of Jesus. New York: Paulist Press, 1973.
(Explores the biblical roots of these two topics.)

* Brown, Raymond E. and John Meier. Antioch and Rome. New York: Paulist Press, 1983.
(An investigation into two early centers of Christianity which shows how they and their respective theologies developed.)

Collins, Raymond F. Introduction to the New Testament. Garden City: Doubleday, 1983.

Davies, W.D. Jewish and Pauline Studies. Philadelphia: Fortress Press, 1984.

_____. Paul and Rabbinic Judaism. Philadelphia: Fortress Press, 4th ed., 1980.

Dunn, James D.G. "The Incident at Antioch (Gal. 2:11-18)." Journal for the Study of New Testament, 18 (1983), pp. 3-57.

* Ebba, Abba. *Heritage: Civilization and the Jews.* New York: Summit: 1984.
(Based on the PBS-TV series, this is a very readable overview of the history
of the Jewish people.)

* Efroymson, David P. "Judaism and the Early Church." *New Catholic Encyclopedia,* XVII, pp. 310-312.
(A synopsis of the relationship between Jews and Christians and the causes
of their mutual alienation.)

* Falk, Harvey. *Jesus the Pharisee.* New York: Paulist Press, 1985.
(Written by a rabbi, this work offers two principal theses: (1) that Jesus
intended to found a religion for Gentiles, and (2) that Jesus' views were
those of the Pharisaic school of Hillel which opposed the ruling school
of Shammai.)

* Farrell, Melvin L. *Getting to Know the Bible.* Milwaukee: Hi-Time, 1984.
(An introduction to the Bible which gives a fine overview of the various
books. Emphasizes the modern critical approach.)

Fiorenza, Elisabeth Schussler. *In Memory of Her.* New York: Crossroad,
1983.

Gager, John G. *The Origins of Anti-Semitism.* New York: Oxford University Press, 1983.

Gaston, Lloyd. "Angels and Gentiles in Early Judaism and in Paul." *Sciences
Religieuses/Studies in Religion,* 11/1 (1982), pp. 65-75.

_____. "Israel's Enemies in Pauline Theology." *New Testament Studies,*
28 (1982), pp. 400-423.

_____. "Paul and the Torah," in Allan T. Davies, ed. *Antisemitism
and the Foundations of Early Christianity.* New York: Paulist, 1979, pp.
48-71.

_____. "Works of Law as a Subjective Genitive." *Sciences Religieuses/
Studies in Religion,* 13 (1984), pp. 39-46.

Jewett, Robert. *A Chronology of Paul's Life.* Philadelphia: Fortress Press,
1979.

* Keck, Leander. *Paul and His Letters.* Philadelphia: Fortress Press, 1979.
(Explores Paul's theology by contrasting various concepts and themes.)

* Leary, James F. *A Light to the Nations.* New Jersey: Arena Lettres, 1983.
(An introduction to the New Testament which provides an admirable
synopsis of each of the books of the Christian Scriptures.)

Maccoby, Hyam Z. "Jesus and Barabbas." *New Testament Studies,* 16
(1969-1970), pp. 55-60.

Meagher, Jon C. "As the Twig Was Bent: Anti-Semitism in Greco-Roman and Early Christian Times," in Allan T. Davies, ed. *Anti-Semitism and the Foundations of Early Christianity*. New York: Paulist Press, 1979, pp. 1-26.

Meeks, Wayne A. "The Image of the Androgyne: Some Uses of a Symbol in Earliest Christianity." *History of Religions*, 13 (1974), pp. 165-208.

_____ and Robert L. Wilken. *Jews and Christians in Antioch in the First Four Centuries of the Common Era*. Missoula: Scholars Facsimilies and Reprints, 1978.

Meyer, Ben. *The Aims of Jesus*. London: SCM, 1979.

* Michener, James. *The Source*. New York: Ballantine, 1965.
(A fictional account of an archaeological dig in Israel which provides a fascinating, though lengthy, reconstruction of Jewish history.)

* Miller, John W. *Step by Step Through the Parables*. New York: Paulist Press, 1981.
(A well-done introduction to the parables of Jesus.)

* Murphy-O'Connor, Jerome. *Becoming Human Together: The Pastoral Anthropology of St. Paul*. Wilmington: Michael Glazier, 1982.
(Provides very keen insights into Paul's ideas about Jesus, which are shown to be highly relevant for today's Christians.)

_____. "Sex and Logic in 1 Cor. 11:2-16." *Catholic Biblical Quarterly*, 42 (1980), pp. 482-501.

Pagles, Elaine H. "Paul and Women: A Response to a Recent Discussion." *Journal of the American Academy of Religion*, 42 (1972), pp. 538-549.

* Pontifical Biblical Commission. *The Historical Truth of the Gospels*. (1964).
(An important document for any reader of the gospels. It describes the various levels of tradition to be found in the gospel texts.)

Rhyne, C. Thomas. "Nomos Dikaiosynes and the Meaning of Romans 10:4." *Catholic Biblical Quarterly*, 47 (1985), pp. 486-499.

* Roetzel, Calvin. *The Letters of Paul: Conversations in Context*. Atlanta: John Knox, 2nd ed., 1982.
(A structural examination of the letters which provides very handy outlines and backgrounds.)

Sanders, E.P. *Paul and Palestinian Judaism*. Philadelphia: Fortress Press, 1979.

_____. *Paul, the Law and the Jewish People*. Philadelphia: Fortress Press, 1984.

* Schillebeeckx, Edward. *Paul the Apostle*. New York: Crossroad Publishing Co., 1983.

(A panoramic collection of photographs of places Paul visited, with an introduction by the famous modern theologian.)

Schmithals, Walter. *Paul and James*. London: SCM Press, 1965.

Scroggs, Robin. "Paul and the Eschatological Woman." *Journal of the American Academy of Religion*, 42 (1972), pp. 283-303.

* Senior, Donald. *Jesus: A Gospel Portrait*. Dayton: Pflaum Press, 1975.
(A fine introduction to modern scholarly insights into the gospels.)

* Sloyan, Gerald S., *Jesus in Focus: A Life in Its Setting*. Mystic, Conn.: Twenty-Third Publications, 1983.
(Presents a very readable overview of the culture and heritage in which Jesus was raised and preached.)

Stendahl, Krister. *Paul Among Jews and Gentiles*. Philadelphia: Fortress Press, 1979.

Theissen, Gerd. *Sociology of Early Palestinian Christianity*. Philadelphia: Fortress Press, 1977.

Thoma, Clemens. *A Christian Theology of Judaism*. New York: Paulist Press, 1980.

van Buren, Paul. *A Christian Theology of the People Israel*. New York: Seabury Press, 1983.

* Vatican Commission for Religious Relations with the Jews. "The Jews and Judaism in Preaching and Catechesis." *Origins*, Vol. 15 No. 7 (7/4/85), pp. 102-107.
(Must reading for any preacher or teacher as these "Notes" aim to correct stereotypical caricatures of Judaism.)

* Vatican Council II. *Declaration on the Relationship of the Church to Non-Christian Religions*, (1965).
(The historic document which formally reversed the centuries-old notion that Christianity had replaced Judaism in God's favor. It proclaims the modern Roman Catholic understanding that the covenant of Abraham is perpetual.)

* _____. *Dogmatic Constitution on Divine Revelation*, (1965).
(The document which formally proclaimed that the critical approach to the Bible was to be employed by Roman Catholics.)

Vermes, Geza. *Jesus the Jew*. Philadelphia: Fortress Press, 1981.

* Zerin, Edward. *What Catholics (And Other Christians) Should Know About Jews*. Dubuque: William Brown Group, 1980.
(A presentation of basic facts about modern Judaism's traditions and beliefs.)

Index of Scriptural Passages

Once the reader has completed this book, he or she may be interested in re-reading Paul's letters in the light of the perspectives introduced here. This index may be helpful during such a re-reading process. Coming across a particularly troubling passage, the reader can consult this index to see if the passage has been treated, and then refer to the appropriate page.

OLD TESTAMENT